The Fugitive King

The Fugitive King

The Story of David From Shepherd Boy to King Over God's Chosen People, Israel

By

Elizabeth Rice Handford

Table of Contents

Chapter 1
A Kingdom Lost

"We won! We won!" the jubilant soldiers shouted as they streamed into Gilgal. What a wonderful sight it was to see two hundred thousand soldiers of Israel march into camp, their flags flying, and dragging behind them the loot they had captured from the Amalekites!

It had been a desperate, bloody battle, and they hadn't been sure they could win it. The Amalekites were fierce warriors. They fought like tigers. But God helped the Israelites, and they finally did whip their enemies. Then they went through the camp of the Amalekites. Everything that was old and shabby, they burned. But the beautiful, expensive things they saved to take home with them. They killed any of the cows and horses that looked thin or diseased, but they rounded up all the sleek, fine cattle to drive them home. They killed most of the soldiers, but they captured King Agag and brought him home in chains (I Samuel 15:9).

They had good reason to be happy, not only because of the loot they'd taken, but also because the Amalekites had been their enemies for four hundred years, ever since the children of Israel had walked that weary way from Egypt back up to Canaan. The Israelites had put all the women and children at the very back of the line. They figured that the soldiers at the front of the line could stop any enemies and keep the helpless children safe. But the crafty

1

Amalekites waited until the soldiers had marched by. Then they attacked the helpless women and children (Deuteronomy 25:17, 18). The only way the Israelites were able to beat them off was for Moses to hold his hands high while Joshua led the army to the attack (Exodus 17:8–13). They fought them off, but God remembered the wicked thing the Amalekites had done. God promised the children of Israel that some day He would pay them back (Exodus 17:14–16; Deuteronomy 25:19).

Now, at last, God was keeping that promise. Under King Saul, the first king of Israel, the army had conquered their ancient enemy. The people shouted with joy as they saw King Saul lead the procession back to camp, dragging along snarling King Agag, like a dog on a leash.

But when Saul got to the altar at Gilgal, a frown wiped the smile from his face. There stood the terrible figure of the aged prophet, Samuel. He had a terrible message from God to deliver to King Saul, and he dreaded giving it.

King Saul pretended not to notice the angry expression on Samuel's face. "Greetings, Samuel!" he cried. "God bless you. I have done everything that God commanded me to do."

Samuel cocked his head as if listening for something. What was it he was listening for, beyond the happy shouts of the soldiers and the people? He could hear the bleating of the sheep and the lowing of the cattle which had been captured from the Amalekites! "If you have obeyed the voice of the Lord," Samuel answered, "what does this bleating of the sheep mean? And whose oxen are those that I hear lowing?"

Saul shrugged his shoulders. "They used to belong to the Amalekites. The people saved the best sheep and oxen so they can make a great sacrifice to God. We killed all the rest of the animals."

Samuel's dark eyes bored a hole into Saul's heart. "Saul, do you want to know what God told me last night?"

"Yes sir," Saul answered in a subdued voice.

"Saul, do you remember how you became king?"

Sure he remembered! He'd been looking for his father's lost donkeys. He went to the town where the prophet Samuel lived to ask him if he could help find them. Samuel told him where they were, but then told him that God had chosen him to be Israel's first king. Saul was aghast. "Me? King of Israel? Oh, no, not me! I'm from the littlest tribe in Israel, and my family is the most unimportant family in the tribe. God couldn't want me to be a king." But Samuel assured him that was exactly God's plan. He anointed him with precious ointment and pronounced him king. But when Samuel came to present Saul to all the people, he couldn't find him. Saul was so scared, he was hiding behind the baggage! (I Samuel 9:1–10:22). Yes, Saul remembered how God had made him king.

Samuel said, "When you were little in your own sight, God made you king over Israel. Now, did God give you a job to do?"

"Yes sir, He told me to kill the Amalekites."

"Why didn't you do it?"

"Oh, but I did. I destroyed almost everything. We just saved the best things to make a sacrifice to God."

"But, Saul, which does God want? Your sacrifices or your obedience?"

Saul hung his head.

Samuel continued, "Can't you see it's better to do exactly what God says than it is to make Him a gift of anything in the world? God doesn't want your gifts if you won't obey Him."

Saul scowled. "I was just trying to please Him."

"Oh, Saul," Samuel said, "can't you see you are really doing only what you want? Rebellion is as bad a sin as witchcraft. Being stubborn is as bad as falling down before an idol to worship it." Samuel's voice dropped to a whisper. 'Saul, because you have rejected the word of the Lord, He has rejected you from being king!' (I Samuel 15:22, 23).

"I've done wrong. I admit it," Saul said. "I broke the commandment of the Lord because I was afraid of the people. But that's not very important. Come on back and make the sacrifice for me so I won't be embarrassed in front of the people."

"Not important?" Samuel echoed. As Samuel turned away, Saul grabbed his mantle, and it tore. "Just like this mantle is torn, God has torn your kingdom away from you. He will give it to someone who is better than you. God doesn't lie. He's not a man. He won't change His mind. You have lost the kingdom forever!"

You'd have thought that at such awful words King Saul would have fallen to his knees to say he was sorry. But he only tugged at Samuel's arm. "Please pretend to the people that everything is all right. Honor me before the people. Don't mess everything up. Please go ahead and make the sacrifice for me." So Samuel turned again after Saul, and Saul worshiped.

But Samuel had to carry out God's command. He had to do what King Saul should have done. He turned to the soldiers. "Bring King Agag here."

King Agag smirked when the soldiers came for him. Though he had murdered hundreds of innocent babies, he thought he was safe. *They won't kill me now,* he thought. He

4

walked prissily up to the prophet Samuel.

"King Agag," Samuel said, "because you have killed thousands of innocent people, God has commanded that you die."

King Agag fell by Samuel's sword, and a four hundred year-old promise made by God had been kept.

King Saul marched back to his palace at Gibeah. If he was worried about what the prophet Samuel had said, he didn't show it. It didn't seem to matter that he had disobeyed God and led all the people to disobey Him as well.

The heartbroken Samuel went back to his home in Ramah. He never saw King Saul again face to face (I Samuel 15:35). Samuel grieved day after day about King Saul. If Saul could not be king, who would lead the nation? It would take a giant of a man, strong, famous, powerful. Israel had many terrible enemies. They would need a great man to lead them. Samuel couldn't think of a single man in the whole kingdom who could do it!

But the loving, searching eye of God was on a little boy in a small town called Bethlehem, down on the southern edge of the country. There were no visions of gold crowns or kingdoms in this child's bright mind. David, son of Jesse, was thinking about one thing: feeding his flock of hungry sheep.

5

Chapter 2
The Boy Shepherd Heads
for the Wilderness

The nation of Israel was ringed all about with enemies: the Moabites, Amalekites, the Ammonites. Why, the Philistines had marched right into the center of the country and built themselves forts! They'd swarm out of their forts into the countryside, stealing food and animals from the Israelites, then hole up again (I Samuel 13:17, 18).

King Saul was working to build up his army. Every time he saw a brave young man, he'd take him into the army (I Samuel 14:52). Of course, King Saul was not very prosperous. Ever since Saul had disobeyed God by sparing old King Agag, God had refused to talk to him. How frightening it was to have enemies surrounding the country and to fear that God was not going to help!

But the young boy who stood before his father in Bethlehem that day was not thinking about the terrible danger his country was in. He was worried about his sheep, and he had a plan to save them. He left his huge flock out in the pastures with a servant boy and ran into the city of Bethlehem-Ephratah to talk it over with his father.

"Dad, there's just no grass left. My sheep are so thin. The lambs just lie about, not frisky at all. The ewes that are about to lamb can hardly walk. I've got to find better pasture for them."

The old man peered down at the young boy. He laid a trembling hand on his shoulder. "David, you must help me pray for rain. Unless God sends rain, we are ruined."

"I am praying for rain, Dad, and I think God will hear us. But meanwhile—I've got an idea, and please don't say no until you hear it all, okay?"

Jesse chuckled. "All right, I'll listen, and then I'll say no."

"Aw, Dad, you know what I mean. Here's my plan. Let me take the flock down to En-gedi. There's grass there, I'm sure. The hot springs keep it warm there, even in the middle of winter, and the grass is always green. Let me take the flock there and spend four weeks or so to get the flock built up. By then God will have sent the latter rains, and the pastures here will be good."

Jesse was already shaking his head. 'No, David. I remember that trail to En-gedi. It's desolate country. Those narrow gorges could hide a hundred robbers' (I Chronicles 12:21).

David grinned. "Dad, who would hang around a forsaken place like En-gedi just to rob a poor shepherd boy like me?"

"You couldn't get those sheep to go through those spooky rocky passes."

"Dad, my sheep will follow me anywhere I take them."

"What would they eat and drink on the way down? It would take you a week to get there."

David pulled out a piece of parchment. "I have it figured out. I remember where the water holes are. They could walk half a day and get to water and browse the rest of the day."

"How would you guard them at night?"

8

'It wouldn't be a problem in En-gedi. It's full of caves. I could barricade the entrance to the cave and sleep there myself. They couldn't get hurt inside the cave' (I Samuel 24:1–3).

"But on the way down?"

"Send a servant boy with me. We'll take turns guarding the sheep at night. When we get to En-gedi, he can come home. You could send me any important messages by him."

"But, David, because of the drought, the wild animals will be hungry and fierce. What if a wolf or a bear attacked your flock?"

David dropped his eyes and flushed as if he'd been caught doing wrong. 'Uh...Dad, I didn't tell you because I didn't want you to worry. Last month a bear—one of those mean brown Syrian bears—he tried to take one of my lambs—so I killed him' (I Samuel 17:34).

Jesse jumped to his feet. "You what?"

"I killed him."

"With what?"

"My hands."

"Who helped you?"

"Well, the Lord was with me."

"You killed a bear and didn't tell anyone?"

"Well, I thought it would scare the little kids. You know how they are. I think it was the only bear in these parts. I didn't think there was any more danger."

A tear trickled down the wrinkled old face. "Ah, lad, surely the God of Heaven has His hand on you! A bear! With your bare hands!" The old man shut his eyes, as if to blot out the frightening sight. "All right, you've convinced

9

me you can handle robbers, Philistines and bears...but won't you be lonely?"

David laughed. "I'm used to being alone, Dad. I have lots to do too. My sheep take lots of time to doctor and keep well. I've invented a new harp too, and I'd like to try it out (Amos 6:5). And when I went to Nob last time, Ahimelech the priest let me copy some of the Law of God. I need to memorize that. No, I won't have time to be lonely."

"Want one of your big brothers along?"

David shook his head. 'No sir, they don't think sheep-tending is much of a job for a man' (I Samuel 17:28).

"They're wrong," Jesse answered promptly. "You've done a man's job building up your flock."

"Thanks, Dad. Then it's all settled? I can go?"

"You may go. I'll instruct the servants about the food you'll need. Say, David, would you like your nephew, Joab, to go along?"

"Joab? Wow, that would be great!"

"Fine. I'll try to arrange it with his mother."

"Dad, promise me you won't worry?"

Jesse snorted. "I'll promise nothing of the sort. All the time you are gone, your mother will be telling me about all the dangers you are facing; and while I'm telling her not to worry, I'll be thinking of a hundred dangers she hasn't thought of!"

"I promise to be careful, Dad. And God will be with us. I'll see you by the second full moon, home with a flock of fat, sassy sheep."

But at that moment, crouched on a flat stone above the

narrow pass into En-gedi, a young lion lay in wait. He had not eaten for three days, and hunger gnawed at him. His fierce tawny eyes glinted in the sunlight as he searched the horizon for some young, tender thing to satisfy his hunger.

Chapter 3
Stalked by a Wild Beast

David and Joab checked the list of supplies for the trip down to En-gedi. They loaded each item carefully onto the back of the pack donkey. Plenty of food? Dried raisins, dates, figs, honey, cheese, dried beans, barley, parched corn—yes, they had enough food to last more than a month, even if they found no fresh fruits down at En-gedi. But, boy, what wonderful fruits usually grew at En-gedi: apricots, tangerines, pomegranates, figs and dates! Yes, they'd have plenty to eat. But David's father was taking no chances. He wanted them to have enough food, so they packed it onto the patient donkey.

Then they'd need plenty of olive oil too. They'd use it for ointment on the cuts and scratches the sheep were sure to get when they wandered away from the flock into the thorns. They'd use oil too for making their bread and cooking their food. When they needed a light at night, they'd pour olive oil into their little clay lamps.

Extra clothes were on the list as well. It might get very cold out in the wilderness, so David put in a couple of extra cloaks, and a warm blanket. On top of that, David tied his new harp and the precious parchment on which he'd copied the Word of God. He slid his sling into his belt, ready for instant use.

They left in good spirits on a bright, dry, wind-swept day. It seemed as if they were going on a picnic. The flock

13

was on familiar ground. They browsed contentedly and followed willingly. David and Joab chatted as they walked. Once in a while one of them would break off in the middle of a sentence and dart after a straying sheep. They reached the first watering place in plenty of time. That night the flock settled down quickly. It was David's turn first that night to stay awake to watch the flock. He spent the time gazing at the stars and thinking long and solemn thoughts about the great God who had made them (Psalm 8:3; 19:1–3).

But day by day, as they got further from home, the going became more difficult. The wind shifted. Gray clouds hid the face of the sun. Grass along the way was burned and seared. The sheep wandered more often into the countryside, searching for tender blades of grass. Now David and Joab had to take turns running after the wayward sheep. They often came back pant-ing. When night fell, the sheep were restless. They were in strange country and unfamiliar with its sounds and smells. David and Joab were weary with watching when the sun came up that morning.

It was on the next to the last day of the journey that tragedy overcame them. Each day, so far, they'd been able to reach a clear spring of water by noon. But on this day, when they reached the spring where they had hoped to water the flock, they found a grisly sight. The sad story could be read in the small hoof-prints that tracked into the muddy pond and out the other side and the bloody bones of a lamb lying in a heap beside the water.

"Wolf," David decided, looking at the track. "He hid in those hills there and attacked the flock when the shepherd wasn't looking."

"I didn't know sheep would run through water like that," Joab said.

14

"Usually they don't, but they probably panicked when they saw the wolf coming. I wonder where the shepherd was?"

Joab's lip curled. 'Probably ran when he saw the wolf. That's what lots of those hired shepherds do' (John 10:12).

David flexed a muscle unconsciously. "No wolf is going to get my sheep, if I can help it."

"Right!" Joab agreed. "But meanwhile, David, we've got a problem. The sheep can't drink this poisoned water."

David nodded. "It may not be drinkable for days. Let's see. It seems to me there should be another spring, about two miles further down the track. We should be able to get there by sundown."

"But that's where that dark valley is, isn't it? Real high cliffs on both sides? Dark even in the middle of the day, as I remember. How can we get the sheep to go through that, tired as they are already?"

"They'll follow us, Joab, because they are thirsty, and they know we know where the water is. Just beyond that spring is a good-sized cave, I think, big enough for the whole flock. We could sleep there for the night."

Joab looked down at the carcass of the dead sheep, then away. "We better get moving," he said abruptly.

When they got to the rocky, narrow pass which led to the warm springs of En-gedi, the sun was already hidden by the high cliffs on either side. The path was blotted out by black shadows. The sheep skittered and jumped at the slightest sound. They jostled each other and bleated plaintively. David sang aloud as he walked sturdily in front of them, but his eyes darted back and forth at the cliffs above him. In any one of those many caves a wild animal could be hiding, ready to spring down on his little flock!

But even as David thought that thought, a strong young lion hurtled out of the gloom behind him. With a savage snarl it landed onto the body of a helpless lamb. The other sheep squealed and leaped away from the slashing claws and wicked teeth. There was only one small bleat from the struggling lamb the lion held in his massive jaws, then silence.

In a flash David threw himself onto the lion. Reaching around, he grabbed the lion's jaw and forced it apart. The whimpering lamb fell to the ground. The lion forgot the lamb and turned with a terrible roar to attack David. David struggled to his feet. The lion sprang, his great paws slashing at David's head. David swerved, reached out and grabbed the lion's beard. The lion struggled to loose him, but David held on. They tumbled to the ground. David twisted the lion's head so it couldn't use its knife-like claws. Then David gathered all his strength and forced the lion's head back, back, until the neck snapped. The massive body collapsed into a heap at David's feet. It quivered and was still.

David stopped long enough to make sure the lion was dead, not stunned. Then he stooped to pick up the wounded lamb. Had he, after all his boasting, lost one of his precious lambs to a wild beast? Could he gather his frightened flock before night descended? Were there other lions lurking in the shadows?

Chapter 4
The Boy Shepherd Needs a Shepherd Too

David put the wounded lamb on his shoulder. Breathing deeply, making himself not panic, he decided what he'd have to do. The main thing was to get to safety. They could wait for water. David lustily called his flock. He could hear Joab far behind him, down in the canyon, rounding up the sheep that had scattered that way at the first roar of the lion. Fortunately, the narrowness of the canyon had kept them from running too far. David repeated his call, and slowly the sheep ahead of him came back to the path. After a good bit of cajoling and calling, the two boys assembled the flock, counted them and started down the darkening path.

"I saw what you did," Joab said soberly. "I don't think I could have done it. My knees turned to water when I heard that roar."

"Don't kid yourself, Joab. I was scared silly. The Lord just helped me, that's all."

Joab kicked at the lion's body and shuddered. "Let's get out of here."

"Let's do." As they walked, David scanned every boulder, every indentation in the canyon wall. His flock was already frightened and nervous. What would they do if another attack came?

It was not long, though it seemed like hours, until the

17

towering cliffs of the pass widened into a lush green valley. The path led by a quiet pool of clear, cold water. There the thirsty flock drank while David and Joab scouted for a cave that would shelter them all for the night.

"Here's one!" Joab shouted. "It looks, from the droppings, like it's been used for a sheepcote."

"Good!" David answered. "Suppose I explore it and make sure there's no drop-off at the back." Still carrying the wounded lamb, David found a pine knot and lighted it from his censer. The resin sputtered and caught fire. The burning torch cast an eerie light on the rough walls of the cave. "Joab, you've found a treasure. It's dry all the way to the back. No drop-offs. And here are timbers they've used to bar the entrance." David's face was lighted by the torch. "All of us are going to sleep this night!" he said.

(It is good that a loving God hides the face of the future from His children. The boy David, resting sweetly in the security of the cave on that night, could not know that in a few years he would sleep again in that very cave. But next time it would be as a fugitive king, a king without a crown, and stalked by an enemy more implacable than any wild beast!)

"I could use a night's sleep," Joab said wearily.

"Me too," David said. "It's been a bad day. I guess you're sorry I dragged you into this."

"I wouldn't have missed it for anything, David. I think I'll always be braver for having seen you tackle that lion."

David laughed. "After all that bragging I did about not losing any sheep, you didn't think I could let a mere lion steal one of my sheep, did you?" David sobered. "Joab, I...I don't deserve any credit for that. God helped me kill the lion. I really was scared...I really thank you too for coming with me. You've been a great help."

"Aw, come on," Joab said, embarrassed. "Let's get these sheep inside and get to bed."

Soon the whole flock was safely inside. Joab led in the pack donkey while David scrounged the wood for a small bonfire. Then they piled the heavy timbers across the cave opening. No hungry animal would get past that barricade! Joab covered himself with his cloak, curled up by the fire and was soon fast asleep.

But before David could go to sleep, he had to check the injuries of the little lamb he'd snatched from the jaws of the lion.

"Poor little Twinkie," he murmured, running his hand along each leg, checking for bone breaks. "Poor little thing. That nasty old lion really gave us a scare, didn't he? Well, you don't have any broken bones. That's good. But look at that ear—nearly ripped in half! And look at that claw mark on your neck. He was aiming for your jugular vein, but he didn't get it, did he? We taught him a hard lesson, didn't we? And he won't try that again, ever, on anybody's lamb!"

The quivering lamb looked up dumbly into David's face, comforted by his soothing voice. David rubbed olive oil into the wounds, then wrapped it again in his cloak and laid it across his knees. Under David's deft, gentle hands, the creature began to relax. She snuggled closer into the curve of his arms and kept her eyes on his face.

"You know, Twinkie, I've got a Shepherd too—only my Shepherd is better than yours. I couldn't keep that old lion from hurting you, even when I tried my best. But the Lord is my Shepherd. He won't let me lack for anything.

"I couldn't make it rain so you'd have green grass. I had to drag you way down here away from home to find

19

enough for you to eat. But my Shepherd makes me lie down in fresh green pastures. Sometimes the pools of water I bring you to are all muddy or salty. But my Shepherd leads me beside still waters, and He restores my soul.

"You won't understand this, Twinkie, since you're just a lamb. You can't imagine how hard it is for a guy to be good! But another wonderful thing about my Shepherd is that He leads me in paths of righteousness, not because I deserve it, and not because I can be good by myself, but just for His own name's sake.

"I've got a valley to walk through, Twinkie, a valley lots scarier than the one we walked through tonight because death is crouched on one of those rocks waiting for me. But even when I walk through the valley of the shadow of death, I won't be afraid of any evil because my dear Shepherd will be with me.

"You know, Twinkie, you don't like for me to use my rod on you when you run away from the flock and go your own way. You think I'm being mean to you when I use that rod to keep you from getting some extra tender grass. But I know there's danger out there in the brambles and thorns. That rod keeps you safe, whether or not you know it. My Shepherd has a rod and a staff too. They comfort me even when I don't understand how or why He's using them on me.

"Tomorrow you'll get to go out into that belly-deep grass and eat your fill. You won't be afraid of lions or wolves or bears. They may be hiding and waiting for you, but I'll be watching over you. And that's what my Shepherd does. He prepares a table for me in the presence of my enemies, and He anoints my head with oil too.

"Oh, Twinkie, my cup just runs over! It's so wonderful to have a Shepherd like the Lord. Just think! Goodness and mercy are going to follow me all the days of my life, and I'm going to live in the house of the Lord my Shepherd forever and ever."

David looked down at the lamb in his arms and laughed out loud. The lamb had gone to sleep, every muscle relaxed. "All right, Twinkie, you go ahead and sleep while I talk! I'm going to stay awake and talk to my Shepherd heart to heart a little longer."

Chapter 5
Can This Child Be King?

Day after day the old prophet Samuel grieved because God had said Saul couldn't be king any more. He kept praying that God would change His mind. Finally God said, "Samuel, how long are you going to be sad about Saul? It's all settled; he can't be king anymore."

Now the prophet Samuel wasn't surprised to hear God's voice. He'd been talking heart to heart with God ever since his mother first brought him to the Tabernacle when he was a little boy. But God had a wonderful secret He wanted to share with Samuel. "Don't grieve any longer about Saul, Samuel. Fill your horn with oil. I want you to go to see Jesse, who lives in Bethlehem. I've chosen a king from among his sons to serve me."

Samuel knew Jesse the Bethlehemite because Jesse came from a long line of famous people. It was Jesse's great-grandmother Rahab the harlot who hid Joshua's spies in Jericho. She'd saved her family's lives when the walls of Jericho fell down. Jesse's grandfather was the famous Boaz, who married Ruth the Moabitess (Matthew 1:5). Samuel knew Jesse was a good man. Perhaps one of his sons was strong and great enough to be king of Israel! Oh, how Samuel hoped this would be true!

Things had gotten worse and worse in the country since God had forsaken King Saul. Lots of the Israelites had gotten so scared of their enemies that they'd scattered from the towns. They were hiding in caves and in the woods. Some had run to the mountains. Some of them had even dug holes and were hiding in tunnels! Some Israelites had betrayed their own countrymen and were fighting with the Philistines against their own families! (I Samuel 13:6, 7). Yes, Samuel grimly decided, Israel would have to have a great and strong man to save Israel now! Which one of Jesse's sons would it be?

Then Samuel was struck with another thought. "God, how can I anoint a new king? If Saul hears I've anointed someone else to be king, he'll kill me."

Samuel was right. King Saul was a violent man. He was often moody and angry. Once, years before, Saul's son Jonathan had attacked the Philistines with no one's help but just one servant. He'd beat them too! While he was chasing the fleeing Philistines, Jonathan stopped to eat some honey. He hadn't heard his father's command that no one was to eat until the battle was ended. But King Saul didn't care why Jonathan ate the honey or that he hadn't heard the command. He just decided Jonathan had to die. And King Saul would have killed his own son if the people hadn't stopped him! (I Samuel 14:45). No wonder the prophet Samuel was afraid that King Saul would kill him if he anointed another man to be king!

"I'll take care of you," God answered Samuel. "You just go ahead and do what I told you to do. Go to Bethlehem to the house of Jesse. Tell them that you've come to make a sacrifice. Take along a young heifer for the sacrifice. I'll show you then which son of Jesse I want to be king."

Samuel obeyed God's instructions exactly, just as he always had (I Samuel 16:4–13). He walked the twelve miles from Ramah down to Bethlehem, leading the young cow he planned to sacrifice.

Since Bethlehem is built on top of a hill, the men of the town could see Samuel coming. They were very frightened. Why was the great prophet coming to their town? Had they done something wrong? Did he have an awful message from God for them? They trembled as they watched Samuel climb up the hill. "Do you come peaceably?" they asked anxiously.

Samuel smiled gently. He loved these people and loved them especially because God had chosen to honor them by choosing a king from them. "I come peaceably. I've come to make a sacrifice to the Lord. All of you go get all cleaned up and come with me to make this offering to God. Oh, yes, please come to the house of Jesse. I especially want him and his sons at this sacrifice."

The men and women hurried to their homes to wash themselves and put on clean clothes and came back eagerly. Jesse and seven of his sons were present. Samuel looked at them and sighed with relief. There was husky, handsome Eliab, Jesse's oldest. Samuel whispered under his breath, "Surely, Lord, this is the one You want me to anoint to be king."

But God said no. "Samuel, don't look on the outside. Don't be impressed by how strong he is or how tall. I have refused this man. I don't look at things like people do. People look on the outside appearance. God looks inside, at people's hearts. This is not the one to be king of Israel."

"All right, Lord. You be sure to tell me which one You want, and that's the one I'll anoint."

Samuel turned to Jesse. "Please have the next son pass before me."

Abinadab could tell that a very important decision was

being made. He stepped up smartly.

"Lord, is this the one?"

"No, Samuel," God answered, "not this one."

Jesse called Shammah.

"No, Samuel," God said again. "He's not the one, either."

Nethaneel?

Raddai?

No, no! No, none of these!

Samuel blinked. Had he misunderstood what God said? "Jesse, make them all pass before me again."

Again, each of Jesse's sons walked in front of Samuel. Their curiosity about Samuel's business was hard to keep in check. What in the world was Samuel looking for?

"Which one, Lord?" Samuel asked again.

"None of them, Samuel."

Samuel really was puzzled. What was wrong? Then he got an idea. "Hey, Jesse, by any chance, do you have another son hidden out somewhere?"

Jesse laughed out loud. "Sure I do. David—he's the little one, the youngest. But I didn't think you'd want him. We left him out in the field to take care of all the sheep."

Samuel breathed a great sigh of relief. "Well, you'll just have to send somebody to fetch him because we can't sit down to eat until he gets here."

As soon as Samuel saw young David hurry to his father, Samuel knew exactly why God had rejected all the rest and chosen this sweet, eager youngster. This boy was not especially tall nor extra strong. But Samuel could see in David's face such a joy and winsomeness that he knew he would be wise and loving, strong and brave, just because God was with him.

At last God spoke. "Arise, Samuel. Anoint him, for this is the king I have chosen."

With unspeakable joy, Samuel pulled the stopper out of the horn of oil and poured it on David's bowed head. The oil trickled down over his face, his garments and fell in golden drops to the dusty soil. A holy hush fell on the family as they stood in a circle around David. They could almost feel the Holy Spirit of God as He came to rest on the young lad. David would be king, a great king. He would be the greatest king Israel would ever know, until thousands of years later when the Lord Jesus Himself, King of Heaven and earth and Son of David, would sit on David's throne at Jerusalem!

Quietly Samuel dismissed the people. Without a word, David turned from the circle and went back to the task that had been interrupted. He picked up his shepherd's crook and went back to the pasture to tend his sheep.

Chapter 6
Summoned to the Palace by the King

King Saul had intended to make himself happy by doing what he wanted to do, rather than doing what God wanted him to do. But Saul wasn't happy, not at all. The whole world seemed gloomy, and Saul didn't know what to do about it. God wouldn't speak to him. The prophet Samuel had packed his bags and gone home and wouldn't give him any messages from God anymore. The Philistines were getting nastier every day. King Saul was so discouraged, he didn't know where to turn. (If only he had realized it was God Himself who made him sad! God was sending an evil spirit so Saul wouldn't be happy in his sin.)

One of Saul's servants watched King Saul pouting in the corner. 'Sir, I have an idea. Let's find someone who can play a harp well. Then, when this evil spirit from God comes down on you, this man could play his harp, and you'd feel better' (I Samuel 16:14–23).

"All right," Saul agreed gloomily. "I'm willing to try anything. Find a man who can play well and bring him here."

Another servant volunteered, "Sir, I know just the one you need. He's one of the sons of Jesse the Bethlehemite. He plays the harp like an angel. You'd like him too. He's a mighty, brave man. Has good sense, knows how to act right. He's a comely fellow, and the Lord is always with him. Sir, why don't you have David come to the palace to play for you?"

Saul sent an urgent message to Jesse in Bethlehem: "Please send to me your son David who is with the sheep."

And that's where the messengers found David too— with his sheep. Though he had been anointed to be the new king, and though the power of the Holy Spirit was on him, David had gone back home to do the work he had been assigned: taking care of sheep. No one guessed the deep thoughts that troubled his mind. No one knew how he brooded and prayed. All others knew was that he faithfully did the job his big brothers despised.

When David arrived at the palace in Gibeah, leading a donkey laden down with gifts from his father, Saul could hardly believe his eyes. How could this young boy be the one whom his servant had described? "A mighty valiant man, a man of war"? Why, this David was just a boy!

But then Saul looked into David's eyes. David stood calmly, at ease. He didn't seem brash or presumptuous. He seemed to be confident and simple, just a good young man. All the love of Saul's unhappy heart poured out toward David.

Saul sent another message to David's father. "I must have this young man. Please let David stand before me and serve me; he has found favor in my sight."

Of course Jesse consented! How could he refuse the request of his king? So David became Saul's bodyguard. David carried his armor for him. David was careful to stay alert, just as he had when his sheep were in danger. For the king had enemies too, and David did not intend to let them hurt his king!

When the evil spirit from God came to trouble the king, David would pick up the harp he had made. He would strum it softly and sweetly. Sometimes he would sing a psalm he had written. As he played, King Saul would feel happy and refreshed. The evil spirit would go away, and Saul would not feel so discouraged.

One day a sentry rushed in. "Sir, a rider with news from the west."

"Bring him in at once."

The man was breathless from the long ride. "King Saul, the Philistines are planning to attack. They've gathered all their armies together at Shochoh in Judah. There are thousands of men there, sir. The general of the army thinks you ought to come yourself and lead our men."

King Saul leaped to his feet, shouting out orders as he ran. He sent horsemen to every section of the country, commanding all able-bodied men to come as quickly as they could ride to the valley of Elah.

David's three big brothers, Eliab, Abinadab and Shammah, all heard the news and reported for duty at once. They were mustered into the army, ready for immediate action.

But David—! Poor David! He had been the king's bodyguard, but when the crisis came, everyone thought he was too young to fight the Philistines. They wouldn't even let him ride to battle with the king. They sent him home to his father! And when Israel was having to fight for its life, David had to do the dull, unexciting job of tending his father's sheep again. With all his heart, David longed to help in the war. But he did his sheep-watching cheerfully, without a murmur of complaint.

But there was no joy in King Saul's army at the valley of Elah. Thousands of men had answered the king's

31

summons. They'd left their fields and mills to hurry to the king's side. They pitched their tents and dug trenches so they could dodge Philistine arrows. They did a lot of talking and a lot of running. They did a lot of trembling. But they didn't do any fighting, and no wonder! Every morning and evening a great big giant of a man strode out of the Philistine camp and yelled across the valley, "Hey, everybody, listen to me! There's no use in everybody getting killed in this war. Instead of fighting each other in a battle, you send just one man to fight me. If your man wins, then we Philistines will serve you. If I win, then you Israelites will be our slaves." Then the giant would lift his voice to a terrible roar, "Send me a man that we may fight together!"

His idea sounded reasonable, until an Israelite soldier got a glimpse of the man. When a soldier would stealthily creep over the trench to get a look at him, he'd run in terror for his life! The giant Goliath was as tall as a house! He made them feel like grasshoppers when he glared down at them from his nine-foot height! There was no use fighting that man. He'd smash them as flat as a pancake with his open hand!

Day after weary day went by. And no one did anything, not even the king. He sat in his tent and stared into space. Some days, when Goliath would yell, King Saul would stick his fingers in his ears just to keep the hated sound out. But fight him? King Saul would sigh and shake his head sadly.

Chapter 7
Facing the Killer Giant

One day David's father called him from the sheep pasture. "Son, I haven't heard from your brothers for a long time. I'm anxious to hear how the army is doing. They may be low on food and too busy fighting the Philistines to get some. I want you to take this food to them and find out how they're getting along."

David's eyes sparkled with anticipation. "Yes sir! I'll go right away. I'd like to see them beat up those mean old Philistines!"

Jesse tousled David's black hair. "I'm sure you would. In fact, you'd tackle them yourself if anybody would give you a chance, wouldn't you?"

"Wouldn't I, though! Well, maybe they'll leave a few for me to fight when I grow up....Except that, Dad, I really am old enough now. You know I am."

"I know, Son, that you'd do your best, but for right now, will you just take your brothers this corn and bread and cheese? I'm sending enough for them to share some with their captain."

"Yes sir."

"Do you know how to find the valley of Elah?"

"I think so. Wouldn't it be best to follow the road up to Jerusalem and then take that road that goes west?"

"Probably so. There isn't a highway straight across, and you might happen into a stray Philistine. It should be about eighteen miles. You won't land up in the camp of the Philistines, will you, David?" his father asked anxiously.

David grinned. "No sir!"

Early the next morning David left his sheep with a keeper and headed north with his donkey loaded down with food. It wasn't difficult to find the place where the Israelite army had camped. They dug in on the slopes of a mountain. A valley ran below them. The Philistine army was lined up on the mountain opposite them.

Just as David got to the Israelite trenches, he heard shouts. He quickly left his supplies with the quartermaster and hurried to find his brothers. They seemed glad to see him and eager to hear news of home. As they stood talking together, suddenly a roar came from the valley.

"SEND ME A MAN, THAT I MAY FIGHT HIM!"

David's head jerked up. "What's that?"

Just then a crowd of Israelite soldiers dashed helter-skelter into camp. They jumped over the earthen wall and dived into the trench.

"What is it?" David asked again. "What's wrong?"

"What's wrong?" the soldiers gasped. "Haven't you seen? Don't you know?"

"Know what?"

"Goliath—the giant from Gath! He started after us again! I'll tell you, if somebody doesn't kill that guy quickly, we're going to end up slaves to the Philistines!"

"—or dead," another voice added in a sepulchral tone.

"Goliath? Who's he?" David asked.

"Just the biggest man that ever lived."

"What's he asking for?"

"Somebody to fight. Wants to fight single-handedly and let that decide the outcome of the war."

"Has anybody tried yet?" David asked.

"No. King Saul said whoever killed Goliath could marry his daughter. Offered a trunkful of money too. But so far he hasn't had any takers."

"Why?" David wondered. "Why doesn't somebody tackle him?"

"Why?" a soldier echoed mockingly. "That's easy for you to say. Have you seen him? He's nine feet tall. Has a special armor made just for him. It must weigh two hundred pounds. He's got a helmet on, and the rest of his body is protected by mail. He has greaves of brass on his legs and a brass breastplate. How could you kill a man protected like that?"

Another soldier continued, "And that spear! The staff's as big as a weaver's beam. The point on it is as sharp as a razor, and it must weigh twenty pounds."

David stammered. "But...but who is this Philistine, that he can defy the armies of the living God?"

The soldiers' faces turned red with embarrassment. "You don't seem to understand. He's a giant."

Bewildered, David looked into the circle of faces. "But isn't there a cause? Isn't there a good reason for one of God's men to fight him?"

Eliab, David's oldest brother, spoke hotly. "Look, kid, why did you come down here anyway? And who did you leave that little flock of sheep with? You're nothing but a

35

kid. I know the pride in your heart. You came down here just to see the fight."

David's face colored with embarrassment. He kicked a stone with his foot and then said quietly, "Eliab, isn't there a cause? People ought to know that there is a God up in Heaven. Someone ought to kill even a giant if he blasphemes God's name. God is strong enough to help anybody who would try."

The soldiers seemed to slink away from the circle, each shaking his head and muttering, "Not me, not me."

One of them did go to King Saul's tent to report David's statement to him. "Sir, there's a young fellow come to camp who thinks Goliath can be licked."

"Is he a giant himself?" Saul questioned sarcastically.

"No sir—in fact, he's just a teenager. But to hear him talk, you'd think he really might be able to do it."

"Well, send him in, and let's see what he has to say for himself."

David's heart thumped as he stood before the king. The king stared at him, disappointed. He was so upset, he didn't seem to recognize David. He muttered morosely, "So, you think Goliath can be killed?"

"Yes sir, I do."

"Do you want to try?"

David took a deep breath. "Yes sir, I do."

King Saul turned his face away so people could not see the struggle going on in his soul. He wanted with all his heart to let David try to kill the giant, but his conscience wouldn't let him send a boy to do a man's job. After all, *he* was the king. He stood head and shoulders above everyone else. It was his responsibility to fight Goliath.

But it was no use! He couldn't do it. God had forsaken him. But—but could he let a child like David try it? Finally he shook his head. "No, David. You're just a kid. Goliath has been a soldier all his life. He'd slaughter you."

"I *can* whip him, sir," David said, and the way he said it didn't sound as if he were boasting, but just saying something that was true. "Once, when I was keeping my father's sheep, a lion and a bear crept into my flock and took a lamb. I killed them both. Because this man has defied God Himself, I believe God will help me kill him too."

"All right," Saul sighed. "Go, and the Lord be with you...Wait—you'll need some armor. Here's mine. Put it on."

But Saul's armor rattled and clattered and trailed on the ground. When David took a step, he tripped over himself. "I can't use this. I haven't tested it." He began to take off each piece and hand it back to Saul's bodyguard. "Never mind," he said. "I won't need it."

David picked up his staff, nodded to the people standing around the king and walked down the hill. He stopped at the brook that ran through the valley. Carefully he picked out five stones, each smooth and round, polished by the water of the brook. His life depended on those stones. He slipped four of them into the shepherd's bag that hung from his shoulder. The fifth one he fitted into his sling. Then he stood up, and strode toward the Philistine camp.

Goliath swaggered down into the valley to meet him. When he caught sight of David's boyish figure, he burst into great cackles of laughter. "Come here, little one. I'm going to chop you up in little pieces and feed you to the birds!"

A glint of anger lightened David's eyes, but he spoke

evenly. "You come to me with a sword and a spear and a shield. I come to you in the name of the Lord of hosts, the God of the armies of Israel, whom you have made fun of."

Goliath snarled, "Augh! Come on and fight!"

"I will, Goliath, I will, and God is going to deliver you into my hands. I'll kill you and feed *you* to the birds so everybody in the world will know there's a God and He doesn't have to use swords and spears. I'm fighting the Lord's battle, and He's going to give you into my hands."

With a terrible oath and holding his mighty spear aloft, Goliath started running toward David. And David started running—not back toward camp, but straight toward the spear of the vicious giant!

Chapter 8
Friends With the Prince

"Somebody's got to stop that kid!" a soldier yelled, watching David run the wrong direction—toward Goliath. "He doesn't have a chance."

He started to race after David, but others held him back. "Don't be a fool. That giant will tear him limb from limb like he was eating a piece of chicken!"

"And when he's finished with him, then he's going to tackle us. Get ready to run for your lives!"

But David, as he ran, was checking to see that the smooth stone was properly placed in his slingshot. Then he began to twirl the sling above his head, even while he ran. Faster and faster the stone whirled. Then David took careful aim, and with a tremendous swing, released the stone. It hurtled through the air and buried itself in the only place on Goliath's body that had no armor: his forehead.

Without a cry, the giant fell to the ground. David ran up to him cautiously. Was he dead or only stunned? David had no sword. How could he be sure Goliath was dead? Then David saw Goliath's massive sword. Using both hands, he pulled the sword out of its sheath. He lifted it high over his head and chopped as hard as he could. Goliath's head rolled from his body. Goliath was dead! (I Samuel 17:51).

Never, never again would Goliath hurl his foul curses at the living God! Never again would he terrify God's people. He was dead! He was killed by a boy still in his teens, and killed by one smooth stone and a slingshot!

For a moment, the Israelite soldiers were so astonished to see Goliath lying on the ground, they couldn't move. Then with an exultant shout of victory, they grabbed their swords, leaped across the brook and started whacking and slashing at the enemy.

The Philistines were stunned. Goliath was dead! The Israelite soldiers were charging toward them. Wow! They'd thought the Israelites were cowards. But if a little boy like David could kill their mightiest soldier, what must the men be like?

With a cry of despair, the Philistines turned to run as fast as they could up the hill, past their tents and down the valley road that led to their homes in Gath and Ekron. But they started running too late! They could not escape the Israelites! The Israelites were mad because the Philistines had mistreated them so many years. They didn't intend to let them escape now. The highway down to Philistia was littered with the bodies of dead and wounded Philistines. When the Israelite army could find no more Philistines to fight, they marched back in triumph to the Philistine camp. There they gathered up jewels and gold, weapons and clothes—all the possessions the defeated Philistines had abandoned.

David stripped off Goliath's heavy armor. By law, it belonged to him, so he took it to his tent. But everybody in the whole country needed to know Goliath was dead. So David made arrangements to take Goliath's head to Jerusalem to put it on display. Then all the Israelites would know God had answered their prayers. They would know their archenemy, Goliath, was dead at last.

40

King Saul couldn't understand his own mixed-up feelings as he watched David take off Goliath's armor. He was thankful that the embarrassment of the past forty days was over. He was ashamed that he hadn't been brave enough to tackle Goliath himself. But he wished it had been his son, Jonathan, who had killed Goliath. Or maybe he wished that David was his own son. And then he felt a sudden sharp stab of envy. Why couldn't he, the king, be the one who killed the giant?

"Abner," Saul said abruptly to the captain of his army, "what's the name of that boy's father?"

"I'm sorry, sir; I don't know."

"Bring the boy to me, please."

Once more David stood before King Saul. There was not the slightest change in David's demeanor. He was sweaty now and breathing hard, and he kept trying to rub the blood off his hands onto his tunic. But he seemed to be not the least bit boastful because of his brave deed. His eyes were calm, his voice respectful. "Yes sir?"

"Whose son are you, young man?"

Surprise flickered in David's eyes. Didn't King Saul remember that David had worked for him before? "I am the son of thy servant Jesse the Bethlehemite," David answered.

"Young man," King Saul said, "I'm not going to let you go home again. I need you right here."

"Please, David," said the young man beside him. "Please stay."

David turned. The young man who was speaking was Jonathan, King Saul's son. Jonathan was a brave young man too, David knew. Many a time he had fought the Philistines, sometimes without anyone else to help.

41

The two young men each looked into the eyes of the other. A great fountain of love and admiration seemed to flow from one heart to the other. "I want you to be my friend," Jonathan said simply. Then he took off his princely robe and draped it around David's shoulders. He untied the brilliant girdle about his waist and fastened it around David. Then Jonathan looked down at his sword. For years, in all the kingdom of Israel, only King Saul and Jonathan had owned a sword (I Samuel 13:22). The Philistines had not permitted any of the other Israelites to own one. It was with this sword that Jonathan had so valiantly attacked a whole garrison of the Philistines at Michmash. Without a sword, a man's life could be forfeited. And yet, and yet—! Jonathan so yearned to show his love for David that without hesitation he unbuckled the sword and its scabbard and fastened it at David's hip.

Had Jonathan any other gift to show his love? He remembered his bow, slung across his shoulder. It was his prize bow, made for suppleness and strength. Jonathan had spent his young life figuring out the best woods and designs for bows to be used in war. His bow shot an arrow long and true. Without even stopping to think, Jonathan swung the bow off his shoulder and put it in young David's trembling hands.

That solemn day, as the body of the dead giant lay on the rocks by the river valley, David and Jonathan promised to be friends. They made a covenant with each other that they would love each other, no matter what lay in the future. Perhaps they could guess that the future would be stormy and difficult. But they could not have imagined the terrible tragedy that lay ahead for them. Usually, when a king dies, his oldest son becomes the new king of the kingdom. Jonathan could expect to be made the great king of Israel when his father died. But God had rejected King Saul and his household. He had chosen David to be the new king of Israel, not Jonathan. If Jonathan found out that David was to be the king of Israel, not he, would his love for David change to hate, no matter how solemnly he had promised to be friends with him forever?

Chapter 9
An Enemy Worse Than
the Giant

"Goliath's dead!" the soldiers yelled.

Women took up the chant, "We're free! The Philistines are conquered!"

Like flames leaping through dry weeds, the wonderful news crackled through the cities of Israel. David, the young shepherd boy from Bethlehem, had killed the giant Goliath. The Philistines had all left the country. Women streamed out of the villages and towns to greet the returning soldiers. King Saul strode along at the head of the column, smiling at the throngs lining the roadways. The women leaped and danced for joy. They rattled their tambourines and castanets and made up a song to express their great joy that they were free after years of oppression. They sang, 'King Saul has slain his thousands, and David his ten thousands!' (I Samuel 18:7).

Like a Philistine arrow, the song pierced King Saul's heart. All his joy drained away. He scowled. "They say I killed only thousands and David killed ten thousands! Humph!" He thought about it as he tramped along the dusty road. "That kid has everything—my son's love, the worship of the people." He kicked a stone out of the path viciously. "There's nothing more David can take away from me except my kingdom and my crown.

45

I suppose he wants that too!" A tiny flame of jealousy began to scorch Saul's heart. At that moment he started watching every single move of David's.

But David didn't have anything to hide from King Saul. It hadn't even entered his mind to try to take away Saul's kingdom. He was glad, glad, glad that Goliath was dead. But he knew it was God who deserved all the credit. It wasn't David's smartness or strength. David knew that for sure! He couldn't get puffed up or proud when God was the One who had helped him kill Goliath. Nor did David stop to even wonder why Saul didn't have God's power. He hadn't criticized him, even in his mind, for not fighting Goliath himself.

Saul had promoted David to be general over all the army on the day he killed Goliath. Even that hadn't made David proud or "stuck-up." He kept his self-control. He acted wisely and thought out the consequences before he gave a command. The rough, hardened soldiers were grateful for his quick mind and careful decisions. They gladly followed him.

King Saul expected to be happy when he arrived back at the palace of Gibeah. After all, the Philistines were all out of the country, and Goliath was dead. He had nothing to keep him from being happy. But he was miserable anyway! (How good God was not to let Saul be happy. Otherwise, Saul might have thought it just fine to ignore God's commands when, of course, it is never "just fine" to disobey God about anything!)

One day King Saul sat on his throne, leaning on his javelin and glowering at everyone who stepped into the room. David immediately noticed how unhappy King Saul was. He didn't know the cause, but he thought he knew what would help. "I'll get my harp and play it for the king," he decided. "Perhaps it will drive away the evil spirit." So, as he had done many times before, David brought his harp into the throne room and began to pluck it softly (I Samuel 18:10).

Saul glared as David bent over his harp. "I'll kill him," he vowed. "I'll pin him to the wall with my javelin!" He hurled the spear with all his might at David. Unaware of his danger, David happened to move slightly. The wicked, sharp point grazed his cheek. He looked up astonished to see the hatred in Saul's face.

Other times, David knew, when he'd played his harp, the evil spirit had departed from Saul. Perhaps he needed to play a little more strongly. Though he was frightened by his narrow escape, he began to play his harp again.

Again Saul threw the javelin. Again David dodged. The javelin clattered to the floor. David fled from the room.

"God is with him," Saul muttered through clenched teeth. "I've got to get him out of here! I'll send him out to the army camp." So Saul demoted David and sent him to the field. He made him captain over only a thousand men, rather than general over the whole army. That way, Saul wouldn't have to put up with seeing David day by day, and perhaps David wouldn't be so irritating.

David didn't complain. He'd decided a long time ago that wherever God sent him, he'd cheerfully go. So he set out to be the very best captain he could be. And that made the people love him all the more. He behaved himself so wisely, so carefully, that folks came to respect him as much for the way he lived day by day as they had for his bravery in facing Goliath. Saul's plot was foiled again!

Saul schemed and planned some more. 'I know what I'll do. I can't just up and kill David myself. The people would hate me—and he's been mighty loyal to me. So I'll find some way to get him killed by the Philistines. Let's see...I'll tell him he can marry my daughter Merab if he'll just fight the Philistines for me. Old Goliath has four brothers still living down in Gath, every one of them as big as Goliath was. Maybe they will kill David in revenge for his killing their brother. After all, if the giants kill David, nobody can blame me for it' (II Samuel 21:15–22; I Chronicles 20:4–8).

When David came into the throne room, Saul said, "David, how would you like to marry the princess Merab?"

David flushed. "Oh, King Saul, have you forgotten what an unimportant person I am? I wouldn't dare to even think about trying to be the king's son-in-law."

"Nonsense!" Saul said. "You shall have her."

But when it came time for Merab to marry David, for some reason, Saul changed his mind. He made Merab marry Adriel the Meholathite instead.

That was just fine with David, for if he were to marry one of the king's daughters, it wasn't Merab who attracted his attention at all. It was a certain younger sister of Merab's, Michal, with her flashing dark eyes and high spirit, who caught David's eye. And Michal thought David was the most wonderful man she'd ever known. Her eyes followed his every movement. She fell to daydreaming at her tasks until the servants laughed with pleasure.

'King Saul,' the servants said, 'the princess Michal loves David. She wants to marry him' (I Samuel 18:20).

Saul rubbed his hands together gleefully. *Aha! This is my chance!* he thought. *I'll tell David he can marry Michal if he'll kill one hundred Philistines for her dowry. I'll let the Philistines kill David for me.*

Chapter 10
David Wins the Princess

As soon as Saul's jealous brain hatched the plan to kill David by sending him against the Philistines, he set out to accomplish it. "If I tell David myself that he can marry Michal, he'll be suspicious," Saul reasoned. "He knows how hard I've been trying to kill him. He's bound to think I'm planning for the Philistines to kill him. So what shall I do? Hmmm...I know! I'll have the servants tell him."

He clapped his hands. A servant appeared. "Take David aside secretly. Tell him I love him, that I'm delighted for him to marry my daughter, and that I don't want a great big gift of money for her." Saul was so sure David coveted his crown, that he'd jump at the chance to be the king's son-in-law.

But when the servant took the message to David, he reacted just the opposite way. "Oh, no, I can't marry the king's daughter! He's too important! Do you think it's a light thing to be the king's son-in-law? Why, it would be presumptuous of me to even think of courting Michal and trying to win her love. I'm a poor man, a nobody. I don't have the great reputation a suitor for the king's daughter should have."

Now David said exactly what he thought was true, but it grieved him to say no. He thought Michal was the loveliest young woman he'd ever laid eyes on! She was sweet and smart, even if she had inherited her famous father's rebellious nature. David wished with all his heart that there was a way he could be worthy to marry Michal. But it was no use. It was wrong to even dream about marrying the beautiful princess!

When the servants reported David's words back to Saul, Saul was jubilant. *Now for step two of my plan,* he said to himself. Aloud, he said, "Tell David the king doesn't want money for Michal. All I want for her dowry is that he kill a hundred Philistine soldiers for me. Let him pay back all the evil they've done to me through the years."

The servants turned to take his message. "Wait! I must put a time limit on my offer." If David had to hurry, then he'd take chances. That would give the Philistines a better opportunity to kill him. "Tell David he has two weeks to kill his hundred Philistines."

When the servants brought Saul's message, David grinned with delight. "Wonderful!" he said. "Fighting Philistines is the one thing I can do! Let's go, men." David raced for the door. Grabbing their weapons, David's men hurried to catch up with him.

David knew exactly where the Philistines were camped. That was part of the job of being a good soldier. So he scouted them out, observed the lay of the land and then made his plans. They boldly attacked the Philistines, and in just a short time they had killed, not the one hundred Saul asked for, but two hundred. They brought back to the palace the proof that they'd killed twice as many men as Saul had asked for (I Samuel 18:27).

When Saul saw the evidence, his heart sank. He knew beyond the shadow of a doubt that God was with David. Saul knew too, looking at Michal's face, that she loved this young man who had risked death for her. That made Saul even more afraid of David.

Saul kept his promise. He let David marry Michal. But from then on, he spent the days and nights hating David and imagining the different ways he could kill him.

The Philistines were mad as hornets. That young upstart David had swept into their camp and killed two hundred of them! They weren't going to let him get away with that. They gathered together to attack him. David was now a captain over only a thousand men. But in this battle against Israel, David showed so much more wisdom than all the other captains, they all knew God's power was on David. Everyone throughout the country had come to trust David. They counted on him to protect them from their enemies. When Saul saw this, he became more and more jealous.

(Years later, David's son Solomon said, "Jealousy is cruel as the grave" (Song of Solomon 8:6). That was where Saul's jealousy toward David was pushing.)

Kill him! Saul said to himself. *You've got to kill him!* The words pounded in Saul's brain day after day.

Saul said it to his servants, "Kill him. Kill David for me." But the terrified men couldn't. How could they kill the man God had so wonderfully blessed? Even if Saul threatened to kill them for disobedience, they couldn't kill David—not David, God's anointed!

"Jonathan, you kill David," Saul begged his son one day. Until now, Saul had tried to hide his hatred for David from Jonathan. But today it burst out like an ugly boil. "Kill David for me, please."

Jonathan stared at his father and shivered. Without answering, he hurried to find David. "David, my father is determined to kill you. You must be careful. Please hide somewhere. Let me find out what he is planning. Then I'll tell you so you can avoid the trap."

David ran to hide. Jonathan brought Saul out into an open field where no one could overhear their conversation. Jonathan didn't want anyone to hear him admit he knew how wicked his father had become. "Father, please don't sin against David. He hasn't wronged you. In fact, you know he has worked as hard as he can to help you. Don't you remember how he risked his life for you to kill Goliath? Don't you remember how the Lord wrought a great salvation for all Israel through him? When you saw David kill Goliath, you were as glad as the rest of us were. Why do you want to kill David now? He has never harmed you at all."

Saul's conscience squirmed. He rubbed his forehead with the back of his hand. 'You are right, Jonathan. I've done wrong to try to kill David. I solemnly promise you, as God lives, I will not harm him. That's a promise' (I Samuel 19:6).

But King Saul was not able to keep his promise because he had never fixed what caused the problem in the first place. He'd never confessed that ancient sin of rebellion concerning the Amalekites. Very quickly an event happened that fanned his jealousy into a raging fire again.

The Philistine army (who seemed to never give up, no matter how often they lost a battle) gathered to attack Israel again. David rallied the Israelite army, and God gave him the help to slaughter them. It was more than King Saul could stand! That young squirt David could whip the Philistines when he, the king of Israel, couldn't even scare them! A wild and haunted look glazed Saul's eyes. David noticed it immediately. He grieved about it, for he loved Saul. How could he help him? He reached for his harp to play a soothing melody as he had done so often before.

King Saul sat on his throne, gripping his javelin, staring at David. Suddenly, with all his strength, he hurled the spear at David. Just in time, David moved. The javelin imbedded itself into the wall and stuck there, quivering. With a sob, David ran out of the palace into the dark night.

Chapter 11
Tricked by a Wooden Idol

Through the dark and narrow streets of the city David ran, pausing only long enough to listen for pursuers. Would Saul send someone after him? David ran faster. His heart thumped painfully. Soon every breath hurt. But he didn't stop to rest. He could still hear Saul's javelin whistling past his head and thudding into the wall. When he reached his home, he slammed the door shut and threw the bolt to lock it. He leaned against the door, panting, gasping for breath.

Michal had been waiting for him and met him at the door. When she saw his white face, she knew something was wrong. "What is it, David?"

"It's your father, Michal," he gasped. "He tried to kill me again."

"How? The spear?"

David nodded.

"Why? David, why does he want to kill you?"

David shrugged his shoulders hopelessly. "I wish I knew."

"I don't understand it. You'd think he'd be grateful to you for all you've done for him—killing Goliath and winning all those battles."

"Maybe that's it. Maybe he's jealous. But he doesn't

need to be. The people love him and honor him. And God would help him if only he would—"

"Shh, David. I hear something." Michal put a warning hand on his arm.

David cocked his head. 'It sounds like dogs barking.' He stepped to the window. 'It's dogs, all right—Saul's dogs' (Psalms 59:6).

Michal ran to the window and put her hand over her mouth to stifle a scream. The house was surrounded by soldiers! "Oh, David, you're trapped. What shall we do?"

"Pray," David said, dropping to his knees. His voice shook as he began to talk to the Lord, but then became steady and strong. 'Deliver me from my enemies, O God; they lie in wait for my soul. But, Lord, You know it isn't because I have sinned against them' (Psalm 59:1–3). It seemed as if God Himself were right in the room, listening to their prayer. 'Lord, I will sing of Your power. I will sing aloud of your mercy in the morning, for You have been my defense and refuge in the day of my trouble.'

Michal struggled to her feet. 'David, those men will kill you in the morning. You've got to get out of here tonight' (I Samuel 19:11).

"I think you are right, Dear, as you always are. But what do you suggest? They aren't going to let me just walk out the door."

"Remember what your great-great-grandmother did?"

"Rahab? Oh, I get you! You're talking about when she 'let the spies down out of the window at Jericho by a rope'(Joshua 2:15).

"Right. Couldn't we—"

"Smart girl!" David tweaked her nose. "Sure we

could—if you are strong enough to hold a rope with a big man like me on the end of it."

Michal lifted her chin. "I can do anything to save your life."

"But, Michal, if you help me escape, Saul may try to kill you."

"That's a risk we have to take."

"I can't let you do that."

Michal lifted her hand impatiently. "We aren't even going to talk about it. I'll figure out a way to handle him. Now, where's a rope?"

David fumbled in a chest. "Here."

"Where will you go?"

"To the prophet Samuel in Ramah, don't you think?"

"Good idea. He'll know what you ought to do."

"I wish you could come with me. But it would be dangerous. I'll have to travel at night."

"I wouldn't mind that, David. But I have to hold the rope for you, remember? You go and come back as soon as you can."

"I will, Michal. I promise."

"I'll wait for you, David," Michal said passionately. "I'll wait for you forever!"

(Poor Michal! What she was promising, she could not do. Because of her father's hatred for David, the next time she would see David years later, she would be the wife of another man! II Samuel 3:14–16).

They walked stealthily to the back side of the house and opened the shutter of the window. Nothing moved below. David took the rope and looped it over a beam so Michal could brace herself and hold his weight. After a quick embrace, David climbed out the window. He lowered himself cautiously down the side of the house. On the ground, he untied the rope, waved a last good-bye and disappeared into the night.

Michal knew that the longer she could keep the men outside from realizing David was gone, the further away he could get. She hunted up an old wooden idol, put it in David's bed and covered it up with a blanket. Maybe it would delay the soldiers for a little while to give her dear husband time to get to Ramah. At daybreak there was a loud pounding on the door. She opened the door calmly, trying to act as if nothing were wrong.

"Yes?" she asked.

"The king has sent for David. He wants him to come at once."

"Oh, I'm very sorry. Please tell the king that I am very sorry but David is sick in bed."

Michal watched the departing soldiers with bated breath. They had believed her! David had a few more hours to run!

The soldiers reported to King Saul. "He's sick today, my lord."

"No matter!" Saul exclaimed hotly. "I've made up my mind to kill him today! No more shilly-shallying! If he's too sick to walk, you go to that house, pick him up bed and all and bring him here."

Driven by the king's frenzy, the soldiers returned. They elbowed their way past Michal into the bedroom where they expected to find David asleep. They jerked back the covers and gasped. A hideous wooden idol grinned back up at them!

"You tricked us!" they cried. "You'll have to go to the king and explain this to him. Otherwise, he'll kill us."

Michal went calmly enough. She had made up her mind to pacify and delay her father as long as she could, even if she risked his anger.

King Saul glared at her. "You deceived me, Michal. Why? Why did you help my enemy to escape? I ought to kill you for this."

What could Michal say? She loved her father, loved him enough to know he would regret it for the rest of his life if he hurt her. How could she calm him? She decided she would tell a lie. "He said he'd kill me if I didn't help him. What could I do?"

But all of Michal's efforts to help her husband escape were useless. In a few days, a messenger came to Saul. "We've found David, my lord. He's at Ramah with Samuel."

Saul licked his lips with satisfaction. "Good. Send a detachment of soldiers down at once to take him."

Then Saul's face darkened with anger. "And this time, there'd better be no slip-ups!"

Chapter 12
The Secret Message of the Singing Arrows

"The king isn't going to like this, not one little bit," a soldier said sourly. "With the foul mood he is in, he may chop our heads off."

"It isn't really our fault," another bodyguard said. "After all, we can't help it if God kept the soldiers from capturing David. We'll just have to tell King Saul what happened."

The men stepped resolutely into the throne room and bowed.

"Well?" King Saul glowered. "Where is he?"

"Sir, we have to tell you—the soldiers you sent to Ramah to capture David did not return."

"What do you mean?"

'Sir, when they came to Samuel's school of the prophets, the Spirit of God came on them. They started prophesying and praising God, and now they've forgotten all about capturing David' (I Samuel 19:20).

"They have, huh? All right, send another band of men."

"Yes sir," the soldiers answered with a sigh of relief.

A few hours later (for Ramah was just a few miles from Gibeah) the soldiers came back to King Saul. Their faces

61

were more glum than ever. "Sir, it happened again. The men you sent to capture David are all standing around with Samuel, and they are praising God."

Anger cracked Saul's voice. "Send more men. Tell them they'd better bring David back or they'll be sorry they were born."

But Saul listened in vain for the clank of chains that would tell him David was at last his prisoner. Instead, there was a strange silence. Where was everyone? The king stormed out the door, yelling for the guards. He found them cowering behind the door. "There you are! What's the matter? Why haven't they brought my enemy to me?"

"W...w...w...we were j...j...just coming in to tell you," they stuttered, "your soldiers are preaching with the prophet Samuel. The Spirit of God came on them too, just as He did the others."

Furious, King Saul stalked out of the house and began walking down the road to Ramah. David saw him coming, a long way off. Now what could David do? He had made up his mind he would not kill King Saul. He could have easily, more than once. But it would be a wicked sin to kill the man God had chosen to be king. No, he couldn't kill Saul. He would have to run. But where? While David stood there, paralyzed with fatigue and fear, God performed another miracle. If David hadn't been so scared and so tired, he'd have laughed out loud to see it!

Just as King Saul walked up to speak to Samuel, the Holy Spirit came on him too. He began to prophesy and praise the Lord. Saul couldn't fight. He couldn't even give an order. He lay down on the ground, and all day long and all night long, Saul praised the Lord!

David realized God had done this on purpose to give him a chance to escape. But he needed advice too about where to go. His dear friend Jonathan would know what to do. David headed straight for Jonathan's home.

"Jonathan, would you tell me why your father wants to kill me? Have I wronged him, and is there anyway I can fix it?"

"David, I don't think my father wants to kill you. He would have told me if he planned to kill you. He tells me everything."

David shook his head. "No, Jonathan, he wouldn't tell you this because he knows you love me. Believe me, Jonathan, there's just a step between me and death."

"God won't let you die, David. He's chosen you to be the next king of Israel. He won't let my father kill you. But tell me, what do you want me to do?"

"Find out what your father is thinking. He's planned a feast for the new moon tomorrow. He'll expect me at the feast. Would you tell him I asked to go home to Bethlehem for the feast with my family? If he says, "Fine, I'm glad he could go," then I'm wrong, and he isn't planning to kill me. But if your father gets angry, then you'll know he has plans for my death."

"Sounds like a reasonable plan," Jonathan said.

"But, Jonathan," David added earnestly, "if you think I have wronged your father, if you think I deserve to die, please kill me now. Kill me yourself."

Jonathan kept shaking his head. "No, no, David. You have done nothing wrong. Here, come with me."

Jonathan led David out into the middle of a big field. The two young men faced each other solemnly. Jonathan raised his right hand. "I solemnly promise you before God, David, I will tell you if my father plans to kill you. The only promise I ask of you is that when God makes you king in my father's stead, that you will be kind to my children."

David raised his right hand to God. "I solemnly promise."

"Promise me again, David. You know how much I love you!" Jonathan could hardly keep from weeping.

A second time David lifted his hand and made the holy promise.

"Now," Jonathan said, trying to lay aside his grief, "we have to find some way for me to get a message to you. Let's see. The feast is tomorrow. I should know something positive by tomorrow night. I know—on the third day, you hide yourself by that great big rock we named Ezel. Get there early in the morning so no one will see you going. If I find out at supper tomorrow night that everything is fine and it's safe for you to come home, I'll shoot some arrows. When my servant boy goes to pick them up, I'll yell to him that he has gone too far."

Jonathan rubbed his eyes to brush away the tears. "But if it turns out that you are right and my father intends to kill you, then I'll yell to the lad that the arrows are beyond him. That will be the signal that your life is in danger. You'd better start running right then. Don't even come back to the house to say goodbye. Get going as soon as you hear the message. But remember, David. Remember the promises we have made to each other. Remember them forever!"

"I will, Jonathan. I'll never forget you or your children."

The new moon came. King Saul prepared a big feast. He sat at the banquet table in his usual chair. Abner, captain of the army, sat beside him. Saul looked around. David's chair was empty. *Something happened today to keep David from coming.* He'll be here tomorrow, Saul said to himself. *I'll kill him then.*

But at the feast the next day, David's place was still empty. Saul tried to act casual. "Say, Jonathan, how come David didn't come to my feast yesterday or today?"

"His family had a special feast too. He asked me if he could go to Bethlehem. You remember his father is old, and he wanted to celebrate with the family. I gave him permission to go."

"You wicked son!" Saul said contemptuously. "Can't you see he is trying to take away everything that belongs to you? Can't you see? You can't be king as long as David is alive! Now march right down to Bethlehem and fetch him. I'm going to kill him."

"Why, Father? What has David done to you?"

For an answer, Saul grabbed up his javelin and hurled it at his own son! Jonathan dodged it. He leaped up from the table, too angry and ashamed to eat another bite.

Early on the morning of the third day, Jonathan went to the field where he had promised to meet David. He knew David would be hiding down by the great rock Ezel. Though it was six or seven hundred yards away, he knew his strong bow could shoot an arrow that distance.

"Get ready!" Jonathan said to the little boy who picked up his arrows for him. Jonathan laid an arrow to the bow, pulled back the string, and an arrow pierced through the morning air. The little boy raced for it. "Further!" Jonathan yelled. "Go on! The arrows are beyond you. Hurry! Don't stop!"

But his words were for David, hiding in a cleft of the great rock. David heard his urgent words. He understood the secret message of the singing arrows. King Saul was trying to kill him! He had to hurry. He couldn't wait. He had to get away just as fast as he could.

Chapter 13
At the Mercy of the Philistines

Jonathan had intended to let the arrows give David the message of danger. It might be someone was spying on him and would report to the king where David was hiding. But the young prince couldn't bear to let David leave without speaking to him once more. He turned to the little boy with him. "Take my bow and arrows, please, and run on back to town. I won't need you any more today. That's a good fella!"

As the little boy's chubby legs carried him across the field, David came out of the cleft in the rock where he had hidden. He threw himself on the ground at Jonathan's feet. Jonathan pulled him up. They hugged each other fiercely and wept together.

"You must go," Jonathan said urgently. "It's dangerous to stay here another second. But go in peace. Remember, God is watching over us and our children. He will take care of us all."

With a final embrace, the two men parted, Jonathan toward his home and David toward a murky, uncertain future with his tiny band of soldiers (I Samuel 20:42).

The first thing David had to do, he decided as he ran, was to get food for his men—food and weapons. They were already hungry since they had been in hiding for three days. They had to have food. Who could help them?

Samuel? Michal? His own father back in Bethlehem? No, Saul would be watching all of them. David couldn't jeopardize their lives. Could Ahimelech the priest help him?

David met his men at the appointed rendezvous. "I've decided to ask Ahimelech the priest to help us. I'll go alone so no one will see me. You meet me at Nob tonight, after dark, outside the town. I've thought of a place we can hide where Saul won't think to look for us. Where? I'll tell you later. Let's get some food first."

But Ahimelech trembled when David walked into the Tabernacle at Nob. 'What's wrong? Why did you come by yourself? Where are your soldiers?' (I Samuel 21:1).

David realized suddenly why Ahimelech was frightened. If Saul thought Ahimelech had helped David to escape, he'd kill him too! David couldn't tell Ahimelech about the danger he was in, for Ahimelech's sake. "The king sent me on a secret errand," he lied. "I had to leave quickly. I've made an appointment to meet my soldiers later. I left in such a hurry that I didn't even have time to get food for them. Do you have some bread you could spare?"

Ahimelech shook his head.

"What about the shewbread?" David asked. He knew that every Sabbath day, the priests baked fresh bread and put it on the table of shewbread in the Tabernacle. It was to be an object lesson for the people who came to the Tabernacle to worship, to show them that Jesus would be the Bread of Life and they'd never be hungry if they trusted Him (Numbers 4:7; John 6:35).

"That's holy bread," Ahimelech answered quickly. "I couldn't give you that." Then he saw the look of desperation in David's eyes. "Well, I guess I could. If your young men have been acting right and not breaking

God's commandments, maybe it would be all right."

"Yes, yes," David answered eagerly, "they are good, clean young men. I don't let them run wild, not even when we're fighting the Philistines. They are trying to serve the Lord, and the bread will save our lives."

"All right, then," Ahimelech said, "take the bread." He began to pack the bread into baskets for David. A thousand years later, the Lord Jesus said Ahimelech had made the right decision. It was right for Ahimelech to give the bread to David. God made the rule about the Sabbath to help people, not hurt them (Mark 2:25–27).

David became aware of the sinister eyes of a dark-skinned man staring at him from across the Tabernacle. David recognized him at once. It was Doeg the Edomite, the head of King Saul's herdsmen! *Oh, no! Doeg will tell King Saul I was here!* Nervously, David pulled Ahimelech into a corner so Doeg couldn't overhear the rest of the conversation. "Do you have a spear or a sword? I left mine behind because the king's business required haste."

Ahimelech stared at David. "A sword? What would I need a sword for?" And then he remembered. "Oh, yes, David, we do have a sword here—Goliath's sword."

David's eyes lighted with pleasure. "Ah, there's no sword like that!"

"You have a right to it," Ahimelech said. "You risked your life to kill him. Here, it's behind the ephod, wrapped in a cloth. Are you sure it isn't too big? It's the only weapon we have here."

"It's just exactly what I need, sir. Thank you, and may God reward you for all you've done this day." (It was a mercy of God that David couldn't see into the future!)

As quietly as possible, David slipped into the dusk,

carrying the bread and Goliath's great sword. His faithful men were waiting for him outside the town wall. They gasped when David told him of a place they could go where Saul would not look for them: Gath.

"Gath?"

"Goliath's hometown?"

"The main city of the Philistines? They'll eat us up alive!"

"No, wait; think about it," David said reasonably. "Where's the last place on earth Saul would look for us?"

"With the Philistines? Well, maybe—but—"

"Right. So that's where we'll go."

"But the Philistines won't forget you killed Goliath."

"They may be glad to have us on their side for a change!" David answered triumphantly.

And that's exactly the way it turned out. Achish, king of Gath, was delighted to have David and his men in his city (I Samuel 21:10).

But King Achish's servants weren't glad to have the man who killed Goliath loose in their town! They were frightened.

"Look, King Achish, can't you understand? This is David, the king of the Israelites! This is the man the women sang about after he killed Goliath. They said Saul killed thousands but David killed ten thousands. King, you're crazy if you let that man stay here!"

King Achish began to eye David suspiciously. Come to think of it, how come David had wanted to come to Gath? What if he intended to kill them and so win back King Saul's friendship? King Achish tightened his bodyguard and began to watch David's every move.

Chapter 14
A Priceless Cup of Water

King Achish eyed David gloomily. Was David his friend? Or was he a spy sent by his enemy, King Saul? Did David plan to regain Saul's friendship by betraying the Philistines?

The men of Gath saw their king's uncertainty. They ringed around David and began to taunt and curse him. David looked at their twisted, hate-filled faces, and he knew he did not have a friend he could depend on among them.

"Leave him alone," the king commanded. "I'll decide later what to do."

That night David lay on his pallet and wondered what would happen. He was afraid—more afraid than he'd ever been: more afraid than when he'd fought the lion, more afraid than when he'd faced Goliath's sword. He was so tired of running, so tired of living in fear, so homesick. How would it all end? Was he going to die after all at the hands of the Philistines?

David struggled to his knees and began to pray. 'Be merciful unto me, O God, for man would swallow me up; he fighting daily oppresses me....They be many that fight against me, O Thou most High. What time I am afraid, I will trust in Thee' (Psalm 56:1–3). David reached for a writing reed and began to write down his prayer. The

Holy Spirit filled his fear-laden heart, and the words began to flow.

'In God have I put my trust,' he wrote. 'I will not be afraid what man can do unto me....For Thou hast delivered my soul from death; wilt not Thou deliver my feet from falling, that I may walk before God in the light of the living?' David began to realize God would rescue him from this trap, just as He always had. He fell asleep with a smile on his face. And when the sun came up in the morning, David had a bold plan for his escape already in mind. Since he couldn't expect help from anyone else and since he couldn't fight the Philistines all by himself, he had to find another way. *Suppose I can trick them into letting me loose?* he asked himself.

When the men of Gath woke up that morning, they were astonished to see David sprawled on the ground in front of the gates of the city. He was scrabbling strange words on the gates. When they tried to stop him, his legs and arms started jerking as if he were having a fit. His tongue lolled out, and spittle dripped down his beard. His eyes crossed vacantly, and he mumbled foolish words.

"Hey, look!" jeered a Philistine. "The mighty David has gone crazy!"

"Whoopee! He's nuts!"

"Ho! ho! ho! What will King Achish say now?" Mocking and laughing, they dragged David to the king.

King Achish looked at the sorry figure crumpled in the dirt. He turned away with disgust. "You can see the man is mad. Why did you bring him to me? Do you think I need crazy people for soldiers? Get him out of here!"

Still jeering, the soldiers dragged David to the city gate and dumped him on the road that led to Bethlehem.

David crawled slowly away, still jerking and slobbering, until the last of the Philistines tired of following him and went back to the city. Then he leaped to his feet and began to run.

Where should he go now? The Philistines were behind him. Before him were King Saul's armies. To the south was a wilderness. Then David remembered—what about the cave at Adullam? It was about halfway between Gath and Bethlehem. He could hide there until he decided what to do.

At nightfall he stumbled into the coolness of the cave Adullam. How quiet it was, and how secure it felt to have strong arched stone walls on all sides! How welcome the moist air was after the heat of the dusty road!

That night David wrote Psalm 34:

"I will bless the LORD at all times: his praise shall continually be in my mouth."

"I sought the LORD, and he heard me, and delivered me from all my fears."

"None of them that trust in him shall be desolate."—Verses 1, 4 and 22.

God had tested him, but God had given him His dear presence even through his suffering.

When David's family heard he had hidden down at Adullam, they all came to join him. Soon, throughout the land of Israel, it was whispered that David had come home. Men who were in any kind of distress, men who had debts they couldn't pay, men who were discontented—all came to Adullam to join David. They were riffraff, undisciplined and wild. They needed a strong leader whom they could trust and follow. David gave them the discipline and training they needed, and soon they were a fine, tough army four hundred strong. Now that they had someone who would lead them, they became loyal and brave. They were willing to die for David, and they proved it.

One night David sat at the mouth of the cave. He was thinking of home. Bethlehem was just over the hills, only fifteen or so miles away. Of course, the Philistines had captured Bethlehem, and he couldn't go there anyway, even if Saul's men had not been looking for him. But David was homesick, and around the campfire that night, he said impulsively, 'Remember how good and fresh the water tastes from the well just inside the Bethlehem gate? Wouldn't a drink of that cool water taste good tonight?' (II Samuel 23:15).

His soldiers nodded, remembering. "Too bad the Philistines captured the town, or we could get you some."

But three young men looked at each other, and their eyes said something very plainly. Did their captain want a drink of water from the well of Bethlehem? Adino, Eleazar and Shammah quietly picked up their spears and melted into the darkness together. "If he wants a drink of Bethlehem water, he'll have that drink," they vowed, "Philistines or no!"

The next morning, three sweaty, dirty soldiers, grinning foolishly, crowded around David. They held out an ordinary-looking cruse of water.

"What's this?" David asked pleasantly. "What have you fellows been up to, and how come you disappeared so suddenly last night?"

Adino, Eleazar and Shammah exchanged happy glances. "You said you were thirsty, so we went to get you a drink. Here it is."

David took the water cruse by its two small handles. His voice was unsteady. "You boys—you didn't—surely you didn't do something silly—surely you didn't try to go to Bethlehem last night, did you?"

The men's faces shone with gladness. "Yes sir, we did. You wanted a drink from the well at Bethlehem, so we got you one."

"But the Philistines—"

"—know there are at least three men in your army that will gladly die for you, sir," they finished his sentence for him.

Tears glistened in David's eyes. "I can't drink this water," he said. 'God forbid it me, that I should do this. Shall I drink the blood of men who put their lives in jeopardy for my sake? With the jeopardy of their lives they brought it' (I Chronicles 11:19). David knelt down, pulled the stopper out of the cruse and reverently let the water trickle into the dust.

Chapter 15
Doeg the Spy Becomes
an Executioner

David's mighty men performed many great and brave deeds in the weeks they spent in the cave Adullam. But every day their danger increased. His four hundred men were brave and capable, but they couldn't fight their one worst enemy: King Saul! David would never let them raise a spear or sword against the man God had anointed to be king of Israel. No matter what happened, David couldn't use his army to take Saul's life. But someday, likely very soon, King Saul would learn where David was hiding. When he did, David would have to start running again. What would happen then to his old and feeble parents? They had come to stay with him when the Philistines captured Bethlehem, and they were too old to run by night and hide by day as David would have to do. Where could he send them so Saul wouldn't hurt them to get at him?

David searched his mind. Say, what about the king of Moab? Perhaps he would help. After all, he knew about Jesse's family. Jesse's grandmother Ruth had come years ago from Moab to Bethlehem (Ruth 1:4). The king of Moab might help. David loaded his family onto animals for the long, hard trip around the lower tip of the Dead Sea, past the valley of salt, and from there up to Mizpeh of Moab. It took them seven days of hard travel, and the old people were stiff and weary when they arrived.

David was admitted immediately to the presence of the king. 'Sir, may my father and mother stay with you until I know what God will do for me?' David asked (I Samuel 22:3).

"Certainly," the king of Moab answered. "I promise you they will be safe from Saul's fiercest soldiers."

With a lighter heart, David returned to Adullam. But Gad, the prophet of God, was waiting for him there with a strange message for him. "David, God told me to tell you that you must not stay here in the cave Adullam. You must go to the land of Judah."

Judah? Where Saul was? Leave the security of these caves to go to the place infested with Saul's soldiers? Yes, that was the word of the Lord through His prophet Gad.

"Call my sergeants," David commanded.

They reported at once and saluted.

"Prepare to evacuate at once. We will march to the forest of Hareth at sunrise."

Not one man protested. They had learned to obey their leader instantly, and their leader, David, had learned to obey the commands of God at once. After all, he had seen what King Saul's disobedience had led to!

But that many men could not move without attracting notice. Soon someone reported to King Saul that David and his four hundred soldiers were in the forest of Hareth. Saul had camped in Gibeah under a tree. He sat, clutching his javelin in his hand, as always. His servants stood about him. As usual, Saul was complaining about David. 'Why do you all conspire with David? Do you think he'll reward you? Why didn't you tell me my own son Jonathan was plotting with him against me?' (I Samuel 22:8).

The servants sighed. They knew Jonathan was loyal to his father, loyal even when his father had tried to kill him (I Samuel 14:44; 20:33). But one evil man saw his chance to ingratiate himself with Saul—even if he had to tell lies to do it. Doeg the Edomite stepped forward. He was the king's chief herdsman, and it was he who had seen David in the Tabernacle talking to the priest Ahimelech. Doeg said piously, "O King, it grieves me to tell you that there are some who have conspired against you."

"Who is that?"

"I hate to tell you, sir. After all, you believe he is a faithful servant."

"Speak up, man."

"Ahimelech the priest is a traitor."

"Ahimelech? Are you sure?"

"Positive. I saw it with my own eyes. I was in the Tabernacle of the Lord up at Nob. David, that wicked wretch, came in. The priest enquired of God for him and gave him advice. Oh, you could tell they were plotting together against my lord the king. Why, Ahimelech even gave him food for his rebels and Goliath's sword as well. I saw it all with my own eyes."

King Saul said curtly to his bodyguard, "Bring me every single priest from Nob. Make sure not one man escapes."

The priests came at once, respectfully. They had nothing to fear, for they knew nothing of David's whereabouts, and Ahimelech had not even known David was running from the king that night.

"We are here, my lord," Ahimelech said.

"Why do you plot against me? Why did you enquire of God for David?"

"O King," Ahimelech said, "I have not plotted against you. I am your loyal and faithful servant. True, I gave David food and a sword. I didn't know he was trying to escape. He told me he was on the king's business."

"But you enquired of God for him, and you know that God will not speak to me. Why did you enquire of God for him?"

Ahimelech shook his head. "I know nothing of this. He didn't ask me for advice from God, and I didn't enquire of God for him. The truth is, he knows so well how to speak to God himself that he doesn't need me to find God's will for him."

"You helped him escape."

"No, sir, I did not. But, sir, David is the most faithful of all your servants. Why do you want to kill him?"

Saul's voice grated through clenched teeth. "You will surely die, Ahimelech, you and all your house. Guards, kill them all!"

The soldiers stood, frozen, their hands paralyzed. These were God's holy men! They could not lift a sword against them!

"Kill them, I said," Saul screamed.

But the soldiers did not move.

"Doeg, you kill them for me."

With a savagery that revealed his wicked heart, Doeg set about the horrible job of killing eighty-five innocent men of God. Then he marched to the town of Nob and set about to kill every priest's wife and child!

That night a ravaged figure stumbled into David's encampment in the forest of Hareth. The sentries brought him to David. By the light of the campfire, David recognized the tear-streaked face of Abiathar, Ahimelech's young son. Abiathar threw himself into David's arms and sobbed and sobbed. "He killed them all, David—all! Everyone of my family is dead. I'm the only one who escaped!"

"What happened?" David asked in a choked voice.

"Doeg, Saul's chief herdsman, told King Saul about the night you came to the Tabernacle, and—"

David lifted his hand. He didn't have to know anything more. He already knew what had happened. He covered his face with his hands. "I knew it! I knew it that night when I saw Doeg at the Tabernacle. I knew he'd tell Saul. Now I'm to blame for the death of all the people in your father's house. If you'll stay here with me, I promise to keep you safe." David might have known about the curse of God that hung over Abiathar's family, a curse a hundred years old, because Eli the priest had such wicked sons. 'There shall not be an old man in your house for ever,' God had said to Eli (I Samuel 2:32). That prophecy was fulfilled that day. Doeg lifted his sword against Ahimelech, but none of that was a comfort to David now. "Stay with me, Abiathar; I'll keep you safe."

But events were shaping that would make David's promise hard to keep. The crafty Philistines had heard that the men of Keilah, nearby the forest of Hareth, were harvesting their grain. The Philistine soldiers swooped down and stole all the harvested grain. Someone came to David with the news. Immediately David asked God if He wanted him to do something about it. (Fine, brave David! Whenever someone was in trouble, he always asked the Lord if it was his responsibility to fix it!)

"Yes, David," God answered him. "Go, smite the Philistines and save Keilah!"

With his small band of four hundred men, David set out to do the job that his enemy, King Saul, with his great army, had left undone.

Chapter 16
Caught in the King's Trap!

"Aw, David, you've got to be kidding!"

The other soldiers nodded their heads. "You know we'd die for you, but isn't it a bit foolish for us to pick a lopsided fight like that when it's none of our business?"

David's mighty men had grouped around him. They were trying to get him to change his mind about fighting the Philistines at Keilah (I Samuel 23:3). David was laughing at them with good humor. "Come on, fellows, you know very well we can't let the Philistines get by with this. Those folks in Keilah will starve to death this winter if the Philistines don't give back that grain."

"But why do we have to fight them?"

"Yeah, it's King Saul's job, not ours."

David's dark eyes burned. "Somebody's got to do it, and King Saul can't."

"King Saul won't, you mean. He could, but he's too busy trying to kill you."

"And, sir," another footman broke in, "if we are scared here in Judah, think how scared we'd be at Keilah."

A soldier nodded vigorously. "There are only six hundred of us and thousands of Philistines." His eyes rolled wildly.

"Oh, no, there are six hundred of us...and God," David

said. Then he wavered. "All right, perhaps I'm wrong. Ask Abiathar the priest to come again with the ephod, and I'll see if I misunderstood what God wants us to do."

Abiathar came, wearing the golden breastplate (Exodus 39:2). The twelve precious stones in the ephod glittered in the sunlight. "Lord," David said simply, "shall I go up and smite the Philistines?"

"Yes, David," the Lord answered, "I'll deliver them into your hands."

With that clear promise, David's men took heart. They marched to Keilah and attacked the Philistines. They fought long and courageously, and at last the battle was won. The men of Keilah were jubilant. They welcomed David's men into the city and heaped their praises on them.

"We'll never forget what you've done for us. You saved our lives."

"Look at all this cattle! We're richer than we were before the raid!"

"How can we ever repay you, David? Please make yourselves at home in our city. We'd be delighted to have you live with us."

So David and his men, weary of living in the forest, came to live at Keilah. Soon King Saul heard about it. *He's trapped now!* Saul said to himself. *The walls and gates of Keilah will be a deathtrap.*

David's spies, posted at the approaches to the city, told him King Saul was coming with his army. Suddenly David was afraid. He had not thought about it before, but would the men of Keilah forget David had saved their lives? Would they surrender him to King Saul? Anxiously, David called for Abiathar to come with the ephod.

"O Lord God of Israel, your servant has heard Saul's plans to come to Keilah to destroy it because I am here. Will Saul really come here?"

The answer from God was clear: "King Saul will come down."

Cold chills ran down David's spine. "Will the men of Keilah deliver us up into the hand of Saul when he says he'll kill them?"

"Yes, David, they will deliver you up!"

David stifled a groan. To think the men of Keilah would betray him after all he'd done for them! But it was true. God said they would hand him over to Saul to be killed! Wearily David struggled to his feet. "All right, men, it's every man for himself. If we scatter, Saul can't catch us all. Avoid a fight if you can. Make your way down to the wilderness of Ziph. I'll meet you there at the oasis just as soon as possible."

Like ghosts, David's men melted into the surrounding hills. They vanished with their weapons and their possessions on their backs so there was no army of David's left for Saul to find. Where had they gone? Saul sent spies out daily to trace them. But not a footprint could be found!

Jonathan, Saul's son and David's friend, was a man David's men could trust. So it was not hard for him to keep searching until he traced David to a wood in the wilderness of Ziph. David could hardly restrain his joy when he saw his dear friend. "Say, Jonathan, have I missed you!"

"And I, you, dear friend. I came to encourage you not to give up. God isn't going to let my father kill you. I believe the king knows that too."

"I sure am tired of running and hiding, Jonathan."

"I'm sure you are, David. But just think! Someday God's promise is going to come true, and then you'll be king, and I'll be—I'll tell you what—I'll be your prime minister!"

"Great," David grinned. "I like that idea. Now, tell me. How is my family? How is my wife Michal?"

Jonathan winced, and he did not answer.

"Jonathan, what's wrong with my wife?"

"Oh, she's all right, but—"

"—but what? Oh, Jonathan, what's wrong?"

"She's married again, David."

"Michal? Married? But—" David could almost feel his heart break in two pieces.

Jonathan began to weep. 'My father made her marry Phalti, that fellow from Gallim' (I Samuel 25:44).

"Michal married to someone else? Oh, how could she?"

"She couldn't help it. You know my father."

Sobs racked David's body. "I could stand all the rest—the hate, the fear, the running. But this! O Michal!"

"Don't grieve, David. Phalti is good to her. He loves her."

"But he can't have her. She's mine!" David said fiercely.

"Perhaps some day, when God has given you the kingdom, He will also give you back your wife. God is going to give you the kingdom, David. I know you can trust Him to keep His promise."

"I believe you. And thank you, dear friend, for all you have done for me. I solemnly promise again that I will keep the oath I made to you to save your family."

Jonathan embraced him sadly and left for his home. David went back to his camp in the woods.

Not many days after, the men of Ziph sent word to King Saul. "We know where David is hiding. Come at once, and we will deliver him to you."

Saul sent back a message: "I am going to come. But David is very tricky. Watch him day and night. Learn all his secret hiding places. When you have him trapped, I'll come."

The Ziphites tracked David to his stronghold. They sent word to Saul that they had found it. David's spies heard Saul was coming. David immediately moved his men down to Maon, where they camped on the hillside. But Saul cleverly divided up his army. Half of them circled the mountain and closed the escape to the south. The other half covered the pass through the mountains to the north. David was trapped in a mountain valley with steep, unclimbable mountains on both sides, and the passes at either end were blocked. Saul rubbed his hands. At last he had his enemy in his trap!

Chapter 17
At Last David Can
Get Revenge!

David peered through the scraggly bushes at the silent forms creeping through the pass. There was no moon, but his experienced eyes told him hundreds of King Saul's soldiers were filing into the valley.

A sentry, breathless from running, whispered in his ear: "Sir, we just checked the pass to the south. It's swarming with men too. There's no escape that way." Then he looked up at the cliffs that towered on either side of the narrow valley. "Nor that way either. It looks like King Saul has us this time."

But David only lifted his face to the starry sky. "All right, Lord, they've cornered us. So how are You going to get us out of it this time? You've done it before, and I know You will do it again. Would You just please hurry? You know how I helped the men of Keilah and how they paid me back. And I didn't deserve what the Ziphites did to me. They were strangers to me. I can't figure out why they betrayed me to Saul."

Then the Spirit of God came on David, and he began to pray more earnestly. 'Save me, O God, by Your name. Judge me by Your strength. For strangers are risen up against me.' Then it seemed as if David had heard God speak to him, for he said, 'Behold, God is my helper. The

Lord is with me. I will praise Your name, O Lord, for it is good. For You have delivered me out of all my trouble' (Psalm 54).

Suddenly there was a clatter of arms and confusion of voices from the approaching army. A sharp command split the silence. Someone had forgotten all about trying to sneak up on David! It was Saul's general, barking orders. "Halt!" he cried. Down the ranks other officers repeated the command, "Halt!"

"Attention!" he then yelled. "The Philistines have invaded Israel. Orders have come from the king. We are to go back at once." The hills echoed with the repeated orders. "About face! March!" Stumbling and muttering, the confused men turned in the darkness and marched back the way they had come.

David and his men stood and watched in blank astonishment! God had done it again! What a strange way He had chosen this time! Imagine! The Philistines, of all people, had saved David from King Saul! It was hard for the men to keep their laughter from welling up and spilling into full-throated shouts.

"'All right, men,' David said briskly, 'we'll have to move out again. Saul knows this place now. As soon as he gets rid of the Philistines, he'll be here again, looking for us. Let's head for the wilderness at En-gedi'" (I Samuel 24:1).

"But, sir, there's nothing at En-gedi but rocks and wild goats. What will we eat?"

"Oh, we'll find something to eat, no doubt. There are caves we can use for fortresses when we need them. I've stayed in them myself." David's eyes softened as he remembered a night, long ago, that he brought his frightened flock into a sheepcote at En-gedi. "Besides,

90

King Saul will think it's a difficult place to live, and he may not look for us there."

But it was not to be. As always, and for what reason David never knew, someone told King Saul where David had hidden. Saul handpicked three thousand men to make a lightning dash down to En-gedi. It was a hard, long march from Gibeah. King Saul himself was exhausted by the trip. He turned aside from the trail into a cave to rest for a while. He never guessed that it was the very cave David and his men had chosen to hide in at that very moment!

When David's men saw Saul's tall, gaunt form darken the cave opening, they could hardly muffle their surprise. Temptation leaned over in the form of one of David's men. He tapped him on the shoulder. "David," he whispered, "this is the day God promised you. God promised He'd deliver your enemy into your hand so you could do whatever seemed good to you. This is the day. Saul is at your mercy."

Though David's friend was quoting God and though he loved David and intended to offer him good advice, actually he was tempting David to commit a terrible sin. David crept over. Stealthily he snipped off the edge of Saul's robe with the scissor-sharp edge of his sword. He scarcely breathed as he crawled again to the back of the cave. He grinned as he held up the piece he had cut off Saul's garment.

The men started moving toward the front of the cave. At last David was going to let them kill his mortal enemy! Just in time, David saw what they intended to do. "Oh, no, wait!" he whispered hoarsely, "Don't touch him! The Lord forbid that I should touch my master. King Saul is the Lord's anointed. I will not hurt him. Oh, it was wrong for me even to touch his robe. Stop! Stop at once!"

Now David's men had been trained to obey him. Their lives depended on their instant obedience to a whispered command. But this! Let King Saul go? Now? When he'd proved he would never stop until David was dead?

"Don't touch him," David whispered again.

The men halted, but they couldn't keep their hands from flexing and unflexing, gripping their spears, wishing they could use them.

After a while, King Saul awoke, yawned and stretched and walked out of the cave. He was never aware of the shadowy figures behind him. As he walked down the trail and crossed the valley to rejoin his army, David cried out, "My lord the king!"

Saul turned around. He gasped when he saw a dim figure kneeling before him. It was David!

"My lord, why do you listen to the men who say I want to hurt you?"

King Saul squinted across the valley.

David called again. "Today the Lord delivered you into my hand. I could have killed you while you slept. My men urged me to. But I would not. You are the Lord's anointed."

"David? Is that your voice, my son David?"

"Yes, sir." David waved the piece of material he had cut from Saul's garment. "See, my father? I hold the edge of your robe in my hand. I was so close to you that I could cut it off. You didn't even know I was there. I was so close I could have killed you."

Saul's knees began to tremble.

"King Saul, the Lord will have to judge between you and me. He'll have to decide which one of us is right. I am not going to kill you. Oh, my father, why do you chase a nobody like me? I'm as worthless as an old dead dog or a flea. Why do you want to kill me?"

Tears choked King Saul's voice. "David, you are more righteous than I. You've rewarded me good. I've paid you back evil. You have proved you are not my enemy since you didn't kill me back there in the cave." Saul took a deep breath. "I know now, for sure, that God is going to give you my kingdom. When He does, David, promise me you will not kill my family or punish my children."

David raised a hand toward Heaven. "I promise, King Saul. I promise."

Saul, still weeping, turned away from David. What more could he say? He gave orders for his army to return to Gibeah.

But David turned back to his fortress. He knew he could not trust King Saul. Saul intended to do right, David knew. He intended to keep his promises to David. But Saul had rejected the Word of God. He had lost the power to do right. It was only a matter of time until his army again would be combing the hills and valleys. With a shudder, David climbed the hill back to his fort in the rocks.

Chapter 18
David Becomes His
Own Enemy

David watched the rear guard of Saul's army file through the narrow pass of En-gedi, headed home again. As the last man disappeared, David looked north, toward home. His mouth filled with salty tears (I Samuel 24:22). Back that way was home—but no more did he have a home. Back there was his beloved wife Michal—except that she now belonged to another man! Over those hills lay home, Bethlehem. But the Philistines controlled it, and his aged parents lived in exile in Moab. Across those slopes, somewhere, marched his dear friend Jonathan, an officer in the army committed to taking David's life. Over there were people he loved, people he'd saved from death at the hands of the Philistines, people whose battles he'd fought, only to have them betray him to death!

What a strange fate it was. He was anointed king of Israel, but he had never worn a crown. God had appointed him to rule a great people, but those very people hunted him like an animal. It seemed as if God Himself had turned away His face from him. David thought his heart would break. 'O my God, my God,' he cried, 'why have You forsaken me?' (Psalm 22:1).

Did David know, that somber day, that a thousand years later his Seed, the One anointed King of Heaven and earth,

Jesus, would pray that same prayer because Jesus too was a Stranger in the land He should have ruled?

David climbed back up to the cave he had made his headquarters. Writing in the flickering light of a small olive-oil lamp, he penned a prayer: "When my spirit was overwhelmed within me, then thou knewest my path. In the way wherein I walked have they privily laid a snare for me. I looked on my right hand, and beheld, but there was no man that would know me: refuge failed me; no man cared for my soul" (Psalm 142:3, 4).

The scratch of the pen on the parchment stopped. Then David began to write quickly, eagerly. "Bring my soul out of prison, that I may praise thy name: the righteous shall compass me about; for thou shalt deal bountifully with me" (verse 7). It was going to turn out all right; David knew it. He couldn't see how, yet, but it would!

Not long after, one of David's young men brought the sad news that Samuel the prophet was dead (I Samuel 25:1). For nearly a hundred years, from that day Samuel's mother had brought him, a little boy, to the Tabernacle at Shiloh, all Israel knew that God had established Samuel as His prophet (I Samuel 3:20). For those long years, Israel had depended on Samuel to tell them what God wanted them to do. Now Samuel was dead. The messenger told David all about the funeral. He'd been buried in his hometown, in the family tomb at Ramah.

What a sense of loss flooded over David. Samuel was dead! Now he would never hear him pray again. He would never hear him preach the Word of God. Never again could David seek his advice. He was dead. Then a chilling thought froze David. Now that Samuel was dead, what would Saul do? If the prophet Samuel had barely been able to restrain Saul while he was living, what would Saul do now that Samuel was dead? Would he, right now even, be on his way to En-gedi?

David jumped to his feet and started barking orders. "Load up! We're leaving at once for the wilderness of Paran!" (David always seemed to have a plan for emergencies!)

If David's men had thought En-gedi was forbidding, what must they have thought of the wilderness of Paran! The only good thing about Paran was that it lay a hundred miles away from King Saul's army. God Himself had described the wilderness of Paran as "that great and terrible wilderness, wherein were fiery serpents, and scorpions, and drought, where there was no water" (Deuteronomy 8:15).

In Paran they were safe from Saul, but a multitude of other dangers confronted them. There was never enough food nor water. This was the desert Israel wandered in for forty years, and God had to supply them manna to eat and water out of the rock to drink. There were almost no wells. The streams dried up in the hot parts of the year. They hauled water for their flocks and rationed it even for drinking. Robbers roamed the hills, preying on passing caravans and attacking Israelite settlements on the edge of the desert.

But David never had wasted his time sighing over the difficult things God sent his way. He looked around to see what needed to be done, and he found plenty! All that long, hard winter, David's men ranged the borders. They kept robbers away from the flocks and herds of the Hebrews living nearby. They killed the wild animals. They never asked for pay or reward. They simply did what had to be done. Nevertheless, they stayed tired and hungry.

That was why David rejoiced one spring morning when

one of his men reported, "David, Nabal is shearing his sheep at Carmel."

Sheepshearing time was almost a holiday, a special time of joy when the hard work of winter would be rewarded. David knew Nabal would prepare a great feast for his shepherds when the work was completed. Surely he would share the feast with David's men, who had worked so hard for him all winter long.

David called ten young, eager helpers to him. "Please go to Nabal at Carmel. Greet him in my name and say, 'Peace be to you and your house and all that you have. I have heard you are shearing your sheep. Your shepherds were with us, and we hurt them not. We took nothing from them. We protected them so you did not lose anything while they were in Carmel. Your shepherds can tell you all we did for them. Now let my young men find favor in your eyes, for we come in a good day. Please give us whatever you'd like to share.'"

The men took David's courteous message to Nabal. They couldn't believe their ears when they heard Nabal's answer. (Nabal's name means "fool," and that was how he acted that sad day.)

"Who is this David?" Nabal scowled. "There are lots of servants who have run away from their masters. I'm not going to give the food I have prepared for my shearers and give it to strangers."

David's young men had enough sense to know they were not the ones to quarrel with Nabal. But their mouths were grim, straight lines when they marched back to David and reported Nabal's coarse words.

David's mouth dropped open. He couldn't believe it. Nabal was not going to share any of his bounty with them— when they had risked their lives for him all winter!

And that was when David became his own worst enemy. He forgot that God had said, "Vengeance is mine; I will repay." He decided he would pay Nabal back for his ungratefulness!

"Get your swords," David shouted. "Four hundred of you will come with me. We'll teach Nabal a lesson he won't forget. What good did it do us to wear ourselves out all winter for him? He has paid us back evil for good. I'll kill him! I'll kill him and every single man in his house! Come on, men, let's go!"

Chapter 19
God Himself Takes Revenge for David

"O Mistress, what shall we do?" The young servant standing before Abigail kept wringing his hands and twisting his cloak. 'David sent messengers out of the wilderness to ask our master for a gift. Nabal was very rude to him, accused him of treason against the king. But, ma'am, all the time we were in the wilderness with the sheep, David and his men were a wall around us against the wild beasts and robbers. We were so glad they were there' (I Samuel 25:14–17).

Abigail stilled her spinning wheel. A flush spread over her face. She loved her husband, but she was always disappointed by the wicked things he did. She bit her lip, not knowing what to say.

The servant continued, "Now they say that David is going to kill all of us. He's on his way now with four hundred men. You can't blame him for being angry. Nabal said some awful things to him."

"There's only one thing to do if I'm going to save Nabal's life," Abigail said, taking off her apron and putting away her spinning. She hurried to the kitchen where the cooks were finishing up preparation of the great feast. She looked at the huge pots of food simmering over the fires. She saw the great piles of bread already baked and heaps of dried fruits arranged on platters. She shook her head, looking at the abundance. God had been so good to them. They had all this. The barns were filled besides with all the good things God had given them. Why, when the rest of the harvest was in, they would have trouble finding space to store it all! Nabal could have given David a generous gift and never missed it at all!

Worry made her voice sharp. "Help me make up a load of food for David and his men," she said. "Hurry. Buz, you round up the donkeys. Saddle mine as well. Joseph, count out two hundred loaves of bread. Dan, you measure out five bushels of parched corn. Eber, you supervise the loading." Other servants she sent for goatskins filled with grape juice. Others brought carcasses of sheep dressed for roasting, and others, cakes of figs and clusters of dried raisins.

Each servant ran to do the job he was assigned. Quickly a small caravan was formed to carry Abigail's gifts.

"Please don't tell my husband where I'm going," she said. "I'll explain it all to him when I get home. Now drive the donkeys on ahead, and I'll follow."

Meanwhile David stomped along the path that led to Nabal's house. "What's the use of trying to do right?" he grumbled. "What good did it do me to take care of Nabal's flocks out there in the wilderness? Boy, am I going to get even with him!"

At that moment he met, coming around the curve of the hill on the path, a group of donkeys laden with food. Behind them rode Abigail. A line of worry creased her forehead, and beads of sweat glistened on her face. Her hair had fallen around her face because of the donkey's jerky pace.

She saw David and slipped off her donkey. She knelt in the path. In a low voice she said, "My lord, please forgive my husband for the wicked things he said to you. If I had known your young men had come, I would have given them food." Her voice quivered, and she wiped her face with the edge of her cloak. "Please, my lord David, don't try to avenge yourself. Let God do it for you. I know God is going to make you king of Israel. When He does, you will regret it if you killed our family to get revenge. Sir, please forgive us. Take this gift of food." Abigail's voice dropped to a whisper. "Please, sir."

David was suddenly ashamed. All his anger seeped away like water from a broken cruse. How many times before he had been willing for God to pay back his enemies! Why, this time, had he decided to take things into his own hands? He bent down and lifted Abigail gently to her feet. His voice was low and unsteady. "Thank God you came. I would have killed your family, and I would have regretted it all my life. Thank you for the food. Thank you, especially, for your kindness."

Abigail dabbed at her tears and straightened her hair. Then she mounted her donkey and hurried home. When she arrived, she found that Nabal had already begun the feast. It was a feast like a king would give. Nabal was already very drunk. He laughed raucously and danced until he staggered. He teased the servant girls. He bellowed out crude songs. He told dirty jokes and became hot with anger when the servants would not laugh.

Abigail watched her husband's drunken acts and knew she could not talk to him now. She would have to wait until the morning when he was sober again. All night long she tossed restlessly, wondering what her wicked husband would do when she told him what she had done. Would he try to kill David?

But Abigail could have slept without fear. For there is a God in Heaven. He looks down on the earth He created. He knows when people are wronged. And He promised, in Deuteronomy 32:35, "To me belongeth vengeance, and recompence; their foot shall slide in due time: for the day of their calamity is at hand, and the things that shall come upon them make haste."

The next morning Abigail quietly told her husband how she had saved his life. As Nabal listened, his heart died within him. He became like a stone. For ten long days he lay on his bed. He did not move. He could not hear. He could not speak. On the tenth day, he died (I Samuel 25:37, 38).

A subdued servant brought the news to David. Nabal was dead! It was not joy, but awe, that clutched at David's heart. How terrible to sin against God past repentance! How good God had been to stop David from trying to get vengeance himself!

Then David thought of Abigail. He remembered how bravely she had acted, trying to save her wicked husband's life. How wisely she had counseled! Why, she had understood David's heart better than he himself had! How lovely she had looked that day, disheveled and pleading, her love for God shining from her heart.

David's mind lingered on the memory of that day. He had been so lonely out in this terrible wilderness, far from his home. He had wept until he could weep no more over the loss of his wife, Michal. Would it be possible...perhaps...suppose...what if Abigail would consent to be his wife?

He waited a suitable length of time for her to end

her mourning. Then he sent messengers to ask her to be his bride.

Abigail had always admired David. He was so brave, so eager to do God's will. Someday, Abigail knew, David would be king over Israel. And to think that he loved her! With shining eyes, she gave her consent to be his bride.

That was the beginning of many years of happiness for David and Abigail. But David's troubles had not ended. The Ziphites came to King Saul in Gibeah. (Why, oh, why did they hate David? Why did they continually betray him?)

"King Saul," they said, "we know where David is hiding. If you'll come at once, you can catch him for sure!"

Chapter 20
Who Stole the King's Spear?

David's two young spies couldn't wait to tell David what they had discovered. "King Saul is there, all right, sir, camped on the hill of Hachilah. We couldn't get too close, but it looks like he has about three thousand men with him."

"At least that," the other spy agreed. "They've fortified the place well. Sentries are out, and trenches dug on the valley side of the hill."

"Abner's a good general," David said. "He knows his business."

"Sir, you are going to let us fight Saul, aren't you?" David's black eyes glinted with amusement. "No, not this time," he drawled.

"Please, sir, please let us fight. We could lick them; I know we could, even if they do have five times as many soldiers."

The other spy broke in, "The only alternative is for us to run again. We can't just lie down and let them kill us all. Don't make us run again."

"Well, no," David grinned, "I didn't have that in mind. As a matter of fact, I thought I'd mosey over there and take a look around."

David's men gave a whoop and grabbed their weapons.

David put up a protesting hand. "Whoa! We aren't going over there to fight. I'm just going to look the situation over. Everybody, put your slings and bows away. Ahimelech, you and Abishai come with me. Men, we'll be back before dawn."

That night, under a cloud-darkened moon, David, Ahimelech and Abishai threaded their way through the hills until they stood on a slope of ground across from Hachilah. David could see right into the Israelite camp. He thought he could even make out the form of King Saul, sleeping in one of the trenches.

"Which one of you is going down into the camp with me?"

Ahimelech lifted a restraining hand. "Oh, no, sir, you shouldn't go. It wouldn't do for you to get caught there. They'd kill you."

"Well, I'm going," Abishai said strongly, so that David had to put a warning finger to his lips. "Well, I am," he said again, softly but still adamantly. "I killed three hundred Philistines all by myself, and I'm not afraid of three thousand Israelites—uh, not very," he ended lamely.

David chuckled. "That's good enough for me. Come along, Abishai. Wait here for us, Ahimelech."

Not a twig snapped to betray their presence as they crept across the valley and up the hill. But something was wrong. What had happened to the sentries? Surely they had passed the perimeters of the camp. Why weren't men on guard? But the two men entered into the heart of the camp, unchallenged. David found where King Saul was sleeping. Saul pillowed his head on a bolster. He'd stuck his spear into the ground, close to his hand. Someone had placed a cruse of water by his head should he want a drink in the middle of the night. Close by King Saul lay Abner, his general, snoring gently. It was unbelievable! Every person in King Saul's camp was sound asleep, unconscious of any danger! (I Samuel 26:7).

The two men looked down at the vulnerable body of the sleeping king. How the memories tumbled over and over in David's mind! There he was, the man who had robbed David of every earthly comfort and happiness. And there, right by his hand was a spear that could end Saul's persecution forever!

Abishai gripped David's arm. "God has delivered your enemy into your hand, David. Let me run that spear through him just once. It won't take two tries."

David put out a restraining hand. "No, Abishai, he's God's anointed. Don't touch him."

"But he deserves to die," Abishai said hotly.

"And he will, someday. He'll get sick. Or else the Philistines will kill him. At any rate, I'm not going to touch him, and neither are you. Here, grab that spear and his water cruse. Now let's go."

Not a soldier stirred as the two men wound their way through the sleeping forms and back across the valley to the spot where Ahimelech waited. They climbed the hill to a clearing. Then David yelled as loud as he could, "Abner! Hey, Abner! Answer me!" The words echoed on the still night air. "Abner!"

Abner heard the voice in the midst of his sleep, and he sat bolt upright. "What's that? Who is that calling?"

"Boy, what a brave man you are, Abner," David jeered. "Why, you're probably the bravest man in Israel. How come you aren't guarding the king like you are supposed to? While you were snoozing, someone could have killed Saul. You deserve to die, Abner."

Abner peered across the valley, his mind still fogged by sleep. "What's that?"

"Check up, Abner. Where's the king's spear? Where is his canteen of water?"

Abner sleepily groped for the king's spear. It was gone! He could feel the dent in the earth where it had been. The cruse of water was gone too. Who took it? How did they get in? Where were the sentries? Was the king dead? Panic welled up and choked Abner so he could not speak.

But King Saul recognized that taunting voice. "David? Is that my son David?"

"Yes, my lord the king, it is I. King Saul, why are you here chasing me? What have I done? Oh, sir, if God has stirred you up against me, then let Him accept my offering for my sin. But if you hate me because people have told lies about me, then may God curse them. They have robbed me of my inheritance." David's voice changed. "O King Saul, please don't hunt me like you were hunting birds out on the mountain."

King Saul fought back tears. "I'm the one who has sinned. Please come back, my son David. I won't hurt you. I have been a fool."

David answered gently, "Send someone over here for your spear. And may God remember that when I had the opportunity to kill you tonight, I didn't."

Saul raised a hand in farewell. "God bless you, David. You will be a great man. Someday you will prevail."

And once again, King Saul marched his troops back home, saved from certain death at the hand of his wronged servant.

But David was not fooled. Though Saul had promised David he would never try again to kill him, David knew he could not keep his promise. "I know that someday I will die by Saul's hand. There is no place I can hide except with the Philistines."

"Not there, David. The Philistines nearly killed you the last time you were there."

"There is nowhere else on earth I can go," David answered sadly.

His six hundred faithful men surged around him. 'Then we will go with you, even if it means we die with you' (I Samuel 27:1,2).

Chapter 21
David Gives Up a Dream

Through bushy, lowered eyebrows, the king of Gath eyed David stonily. "You've come back."

"Yes sir. I found out I couldn't stay away," David answered with a trace of a grin.

"Pooh!" Achish said morosely. "You played a dirty trick on me the last time you were in Gath."

"Because I pretended to be crazy? Maybe I was crazy! You would have been too if your soldiers had you surrounded and were threatening to test their sharp swords on your skin!"

A smile cracked King Achish's face. "Well, you are here, anyway, however you left."

"Yes sir, all six hundred of us are here. May we stay?"

"Does King Saul know you are here?"

"I'm sure it has been reported to him, sir. Every move I've made for five years has been."

"Well, you are safe from Saul here in Gath."

David chuckled. "Right. King Saul won't likely tackle your army very soon."

"I wish he'd try. We'd smash him to bits. We've never been in better shape. Mark my words, David. Someday King Saul must face us in battle."

David looked steadily into the king's eyes. "And on that day, may God's will be done."

King Achish matched his look evenly. Then, as if he had learned from David's expression what he wanted to know, he said, "So be it. You and your men are welcome to stay. The royal city is yours."

"I fear we will crowd you, sir. Why not give us a place out in the country?"

"All right," the king answered. "You may have Ziklag. It's only twenty miles away. It's close enough that you could get to Gath in a hurry if I needed you. It's a nice place but needs lots of work—just the kind of thing your men could do."

"That would be splendid." David saluted. "I'll report back as soon as we get settled."

How wonderful it was to David and his men to settle down at last after years of running and hiding! The men built homes for their families. They planted crops. They began to establish herds of cattle and flocks of sheep.

Nevertheless they often grieved. They could see vicious bands of robbers riding into the land of Israel, looting and stealing. The Geshurites, the Gezrites and the Amalekites would attack an Israelite town and rob it of everything of value. (Years before, King Saul hadn't destroyed the Amalekites as God had commanded. Now they were a continual source of misery to the Jews living in the frontier towns. I Samuel 15:18, 19.) Now, Saul and his army could not stop them. God had forsaken Saul. God would not listen to his prayers. He would not tell him what to do. If Israel were to be delivered from her enemies, David would have to do it, even if he was a fugitive and exiled from home.

David had to plan his strategy carefully. King Achish

trusted him, but the other Philistines didn't (I Samuel 29:3). They thought, *What if David is really a spy for King Saul?* Others said, "If Saul really is David's enemy, what better way could David regain his friendship than by killing Saul's enemies—namely, us?" Nor had any of the Philistines forgotten the fact that it was David who had killed their hero, Goliath. In fact, the Philistines couldn't think of one good reason why they ought to trust David!

David commanded his soldiers, "Men, when I send you out to battle, don't leave a single person alive to come to Gath to tell the Philistines what happened." When David sent a detachment of soldiers to stop a band of marauding Amalekites, his men would kill every single man so no one would tell King Achish what had happened and whom they had fought. When David's men captured the things the enemy had stolen from the Israelites, David always shared them with King Achish. David's men brought back gorgeous clothing, food, sheep and oxen, donkeys and camels. Since they were Israelite possessions which the enemy had stolen, King Achish assumed David was fighting with his own nation.

"Where did you fight today?" Achish would ask, viewing the expensive jewelry and clothing David had given him.

"Against the south of Judah," David would lie.

It seemed a simple thing to say. And David thought he had to lie to save the lives of his six hundred men and their families. David seemed to forget that God had always taken care of him without his ever having to do wrong. He seemed to forget how God hates a false witness (Proverbs 6:16, 17). He forgot how a lie can twist and grow and trap you into more and more sin. So David lied to the king of Gath. The day would come when David would rue every lie he had told.

115

But that didn't happen right away. For a year and four months David lived in Ziklag. Month by month more brave men came from all parts of Israel to join David (I Chronicles 12:21,22). In between their lightning assaults on enemy nations, David's men trained and readied themselves for battle. They would target practice with stones. They fashioned powerful bows and arrows and learned to hit a moving target. They could shoot with either hand. They had fencing contests with their swords and learned to use their shields so well that an enemy spear couldn't touch them. They were as brave as lions and ran like deer. Even the flooded Jordan River didn't stop them in their wars against Israel's enemies. Wherever there was a need, there these men went (I Chronicles 12:1–15).

But then, one frightening day, the lies David had told King Achish trapped him. The one thing David had said he would not do, could not do, was to kill King Saul. Again and again, he had risked his life rather than touch the man God had anointed to be king. But because of his lies, it looked as if David would be forced to kill King Saul after all!

Chapter 22
David Marches to Battle
Against His Own King

Fleet camel riders brought an urgent message to Philistine garrisons throughout Palestine: "The lords of the Philistines command you to march at once for Shunem. We gather to destroy forever the armies of Israel."

At once, the fierce Philistine armies began to stream toward the appointed place. They marched from the forts they'd built on Israelite land: Michmash and Bethlehem and Geba. They even had a fort at Shiloh, where the ark of God had stood so many years. They came with disciplined speed from the home cities: Ashdod and Ekron, Askelon and Gaza.

Achish, king of Gath, the master of David, also received the summons (I Samuel 28:1). Holding the decree in his hand, King Achish announced to David, "David, we are marching at once to fight Israel."

Not a muscle twitched to betray David's emotions. "Yes sir."

"Assuredly, you will go out to battle with me, you *and* your men."

"Sir, you know what your servant can do," David answered evenly.

"Yes, David, I am well aware of your faithfulness and

your ability. That's why I have made you my bodyguard forever. Now go mobilize your men. We must leave at daybreak."

David sped home to Ziklag. His mind was whirling. He was trapped, trapped by his own lies!

What was he going to do? He had sacrificed his home, the comfort of his family, all the joys of living in his own country, all for one thing: so he would not hurt King Saul. Not only had he sworn to Saul that he would not kill him, he had made a solemn vow to his friend Jonathan that he would not touch his father. More than that, he had promised God. So how could he—how *could* he—march with Israel's enemies to fight his own people and his own king? What if his own brothers were still in the Israelite army? What if it were *his* spear that pierced King Saul's heart?

But then, David argued with himself, how could he *not* fight them? King Achish had been good to him. He had given him homes and land for all his men. Achish had defended him against the threats of the Philistine lords. Achish had trusted David with his own life. How could David betray this man who had saved him from certain death?

David groaned. "O God, please help me. Please show me what I ought to do." But David could see no way out.

At Ziklag, David called his men together. "The Philistines are preparing for an all-out attack on Israel. King Achish has commanded us to march at once for Shunem."

His men's faces showed their mixed emotions. Hooray! At last God was going to let them fight their leader's enemy. But then they hushed their shouts. They remembered how adamant David had been that he would not fight Saul.

"Where is King Saul?" they asked.

"The Philistine spies say he's camped with the army at the fountain in Jezreel."

"Sir, what are you going to do? Will you fight for Israel or with her enemies?"

Pain etched lines on David's face. "I don't know. God hasn't showed me yet what to do. So we will march as we've been commanded and wait for God to make a way out for us" (I Corinthians 10:13).

"We're with you, David, whatever you decide," said his men loyally.

With troubled heart David led his men to Aphek, where the Philistines from the territory of Gath were meeting for the march to Shunem. David could hardly believe how many soldiers there were. Hundreds, no, thousands of Philistines had gathered, and this was only a part of the total force. How could Israel possibly conquer them now that God was not on their side and the prophet Samuel was not alive to pray for them?

Quietly, David ordered his men to fall in at the end of the Philistine ranks. King Achish marched with them, bursting with pride at their strong, disciplined appearance. David's men looked like real soldiers!

Suddenly a harsh voice punctured King Achish's pride. 'Hold it, hold it just one minute, Achish!' (I Samuel 29:3).

Achish turned to face a Philistine lord, purple with anger. "What are these Jews doing here?" the man asked angrily.

King Achish answered civilly, "This is David, the

servant of Saul, the king of Israel. He has been with me for more than a year."

"Why is he here?"

"To help us fight the Israelites."

"Oh, no, he's not," the man bellowed. "He's marching right back home to Ziklag—he and all these men with him."

"Why? I've found no fault with him from the day he came until today. He's a brave man, a terrific fighter. I need him."

"But he is a servant of King Saul."

"You know Saul has been trying to kill him for years."

"And so Saul is mad at him. What's the best way for him to regain Saul's friendship? By chopping off our heads like he did Goliath's, that's how." The man gasped for breath, then hurried on. "Achish, have you lost your mind? This is the man they sang that song about, 'Saul slew his thousands, and David his ten thousands.' I say he goes home; that's all there is to it."

The mutterings of the other Philistine lords made King Achish realize he had no choice. David could not go to battle with him.

"David, surely, as there is a God, you have been upright. I haven't seen one thing wrong in what you've done. Everything you do is good. I have found no evil in you since the day you came to work for me. But the Philistine lords don't trust you. So you must go home."

David had learned not to betray his emotions. Hiding his joy, he merely said, "What have I done wrong? Why don't you trust me?"

"I do trust you, David. The princes don't. So you must leave in the morning."

With hearts full of thanksgiving, David's men began the march back to Ziklag. It took them three days to make the long march home. When they neared Ziklag, they saw a towering column of black smoke hanging on the southern horizon. Suddenly, they were uneasy. What could that be? Surely—oh, no, surely it was not—not Ziklag?

But it was Ziklag!

When David's men crested the last hill and looked toward their home city, they could see nothing but blackened, charred timbers still smoldering. Not a thing moved. There was not a living being in sight!

Chapter 23
David's Mighty Men Turn Against Him

David's mighty men rushed through the smoking rubble of Ziklag, their eyes blinded by tears. There was no trace of their families to be found. Had they been kidnapped and tortured? Were their children to grow up slaves of savages? Had they been murdered? That might be better than torture! Did their dead bodies lie under the smoldering embers of their homes? There were no clues. They had vanished. David's men could not even guess which way across the wilderness wastes they ought to go to look for them.

Then those strong men, who had fearlessly fought giants and wild beasts, sat down on the ground and wept until they could weep no more.

Finally they began to dry their tears. "How could this happen to us when we've been trying to do God's will?"

"Has God forgotten all about us?"

Then one hard voice penetrated their grief. "It's all David's fault. He should have left a guard at Ziklag when we marched to Shunem."

Treason! It sounded like treason—from one of David's own faithful men!

Instead of hurrying to defend their leader, others began to repeat the accusation. "It's David's fault."

"Our children are gone forever."

Someone muttered, 'We ought to stone David' (I Samuel 30:6).

David could hardly believe his ears. For one thing, he had lost his own family too. These men were his friends. They had risked their lives for him. Now they talked of stoning him! *My men could do a pretty good job of it,* David thought grimly. After all, they had been practicing for months. Any one of them could hit a target, throwing with either hand (I Chronicles 12:2). Their hateful words cut into David's heart as deeply as if they had twisted a knife. What could David do now that even his friends had turned against him?

Then David remembered how God had a hundred times before saved him out of trouble just as bad: when he faced Goliath without a sword, when the Philistines surrounded him in Gath, when King Saul's army trapped him on the mountain. No, he couldn't get discouraged now. God had always saved him before. Surely He would save him now. 'Why are you cast down, O my soul?' he asked himself. 'Why are you so disquieted? Put your hope in God. I will praise the Lord, who is the health of my countenance and my God!' (Psalm 42:11).

"Abiathar, please bring the ephod," David said quietly to the priest.

The precious stones of the ephod glittered in the sunlight as Abiathar brought it to David. "God," David asked quietly, "shall I go after the men who did this awful deed? Can I catch them if I go?"

"Yes, David," God answered plainly, "go after them. I

promise you that you will catch them and you'll get back everything they stole."

David faced his angry men. "God has told me He will help us find our wives and children. Will you please go with me to rescue them?"

David's men looked at each other guiltily. Always before, their leader had led them the right way. If David said God had told him what to do, then God had told him what to do, and everything would turn out all right. "Yes sir," they answered as one, "we are with you."

But the men were terribly tired. They had been marching at least for six days, up to Aphek and back. If it weren't that the lives of their families were at stake, they could not have found the strength to even try. But each man gamely buckled on his armor and started across the wilderness with David.

When they got to the brook Besor, some of the men didn't have the strength to go on. "You men stay here with the supplies," David said. "We'll press on and be back as soon as possible."

Once across the river, David could not tell which way to turn. There was no trail he could see to follow. Then David's scouts brought to him a young man, an Egyptian. They had found him lying in the sun, nearly unconscious. "Perhaps he can tell us which way the army went," David said. Carefully he gave him sips of water to drink. When the young man began to revive, David gave him bread and figs and raisins. "Who are you, and where did you come from?" David asked.

"I'm an Egyptian, a slave of an Amalekite. I got sick three days ago, and he left me to die. We were coming back from an invasion of the land of Judah. We found Ziklag unprotected and burned it."

David worked to control his voice as he asked, "Can you show me where the Amalekites are now?"

"Yes sir, I can. But please, sir, please don't kill me or give me back to my old master."

David's eyes glistened with tears. "Kill you? When you have helped us to save our families? Never!"

It was twilight when the young man led David and his four hundred men to a bluff overlooking the Amalekite camp. There they could see the heathen soldiers celebrating, dancing, drinking, gloating over the loot they had captured from the Israelites and the Philistines. And though David's men were outnumbered by the hundreds, they attacked at once. All night long the battle raged and all the next day, until at last every wicked Amalekite was dead. Only four hundred young men escaped on camels.

And when the Israelites hurried to unbind the prisoners, every man found his wife and children safe! Not one person had been killed. All their cattle, their sheep, all the clothing and money that had been stolen—everything was safe. Besides getting back their own possessions, they found hundreds of animals and possessions the Amalekites had robbed from others.

With eager steps they hurried back to the brook Besor. There every single family was reunited. The women told with tears how God had kept the men from killing them. And the men confessed how angry they had been at David when they found the town burned. They laughed and sang and fixed a great feast so that everyone was completely satisfied.

Then it came time to divide up the jewels and garments and herds taken from the Amalekites. Suddenly, the men who had crossed over the brook and actually fought with the Amalekites got selfish. They didn't want to share the spoil with the men who had been too tired to keep going. "You can have your wives and children back," they announced, "but you can't have anything else."

But David spoke gently. "Not so, my brethren. It was the Lord who preserved us and delivered our enemies into our hands. It was nothing we did; we didn't earn His help. God did it just because He loves us. So we are going to divide everything equally. Those who stayed behind and took care of the supplies will share equally with those who fought." And from that day on the people made it a law. They learned that God wants to reward people, not just because they are strong or smart, but also because they are faithful.

David was even more generous with his share of the loot. He divided it up and sent it to people all over Judah. He sent gifts to those who had befriended him in all his wanderings. He sent gifts to those who had been robbed by the Amalekites. And then he set about rebuilding Ziklag.

But one question kept haunting him. While he had been down in the southern part of the country fighting the Amalekites, the Philistines had been marching to battle with King Saul. What was happening up in Jezreel where Saul faced enormous hoards of fierce Philistines? Had the battle been fought yet? Had King Saul turned from his sin so God would hear him pray? Or was he dead? Who was king of David's poor country now?

Chapter 24
The Awful Day God Was Deaf

The night seemed filled with formless, nameless foreboding. Across the hills to the west the last of the Philistine armies had moved into position to attack. All along the low, brooding mountain of Gilboa, Israelite warriors fretfully polished their armor. They were unable to sleep, and dread filled their hearts at the thought of the morning attack.

No one seemed to notice three muffled figures that left the Israelite camp and vanished into the dark night. Silently, unchallenged by Saul's sentries, they worked their way over the mountains to the north. At last, near midnight, they came to the village of Endor.

One of the three men whispered to his companion. "Sir, this is it. The house with the light in the window...but, sir, are you sure you should—?"

The tall man, whose shoulders seemed weighted down by a burden too heavy for him to carry, spoke abruptly. "I have no choice. I have to do this. I must know what to do when the Philistines attack tomorrow. I have prayed, but God will not answer me. Samuel is dead. God won't speak to me through dreams or the prophets or the priests. Yes, I have to do this!"

The third man spoke gently. "But, sir, what good will it do? Why not leave the battle in God's hands?"

The tall man sighed heavily. "We have come this far. Knock."

A woman's voice answered sharply, "Who is it?"

"Travelers needing aid. Please open the door."

The woman slid back the bolt of the door and peered into the men's faces by the light of her lantern. Her shrewd eyes examined them carefully. Satisfied, she opened the door. "All right, what do you want?"

The tall man spoke with effort. 'I need to talk to one who is dead. I know you are a witch. You can call people back from the dead. I want you to call up the one whom I shall name to you' (I Samuel 28:8).

The woman's eyes filled with scorn. "Why do you ask such a thing? You know King Saul has killed all the witches and wizards in the land. Why are you trying to trap me? I haven't done anything to you. Why do you want me to be killed?"

"Madam, as God lives, you will not be punished if you do as I ask."

She searched his face. "All right, I believe you. Whom shall I call up for you?"

"Samuel, the prophet of God."

A deathly hush filled the room. Then the woman's scream pierced the night air.

"What is it?" the tall man exclaimed. "What do you see?"

The woman stared at the tall man. "You have deceived me. You are King Saul himself!"

"I am," he admitted. Then, impatiently, he asked, "Tell me, what did you see?"

"I saw gods coming up out of the ground," she gasped.

130

By her terror, the men in the room sensed she probably had never used her awesome satanic power before and that she was as frightened as they.

But King Saul was too far now in his sin to turn back. "What else did you see?" he pressed.

"An old man, covered with a mantle."

Instantly Saul realized that the spirit of the prophet Samuel was in the room. Though he could see nothing, he bowed himself to the ground.

Samuel's voice seemed infinitely weary. "Why have you disquieted me, to bring me up?"

"I am sore distressed," Saul answered. "The Philistines make war against me, and God is departed from me. Samuel, help me. Please help me!"

"Why do you ask this of me, Saul, seeing the Lord has departed from you? Saul, God is your enemy!"

Saul shuddered and covered his face with his hands.

Samuel's tired voice continued, "The Lord has torn the kingdom out of your hands and given it to David. Saul, you would not obey God in destroying Amalek. Not only has God taken the kingdom away from you, but tomorrow God will deliver you and your sons into the hands of the Philistines. Israel will be defeated. You and your sons will die!"

At those awful words, King Saul collapsed in a convulsive heap on the ground. His servants stood by helplessly. "He hasn't eaten anything all day. No wonder he is weak."

Saul's distress deeply grieved the woman. She pulled at his shoulders, trying to draw him to his feet. "Sir, I put my life in your hands when I did what you asked me to. Now listen to me. Let me prepare a little food for you so you will have enough strength to go on your way."

Saul pushed her away. "I can't eat. What's the use of eating? God has forsaken me!"

The men looked at each other, then looked away helplessly. It was true. What use was there to live if you couldn't get God to listen to you? What good was money or fame or even food if God Himself was your enemy?

"But we can't just let him lie here," his two companions said. They pulled Saul to his feet and sat him on the bed. The woman hurried to stir up the fire and cook him some food. The three men ate hastily and slipped out into the night in time to reach the restless army at Gilboa before the sun reddened the eastern sky.

But by the dawn of the next day, every word of Samuel's dreadful prophecy had come true. Mount Gilboa was strewn with the tortured and dying bodies of the armies of Israel. King Saul and his three sons were dead, their bodies hung on the walls of Bethshan to be mutilated and mocked by the Philistines. King Saul's armor was taken to the temple of the Philistine false god to be flaunted in an atempt to exalt their god over the great God Jehovah, Israel's God and the Holy Creator of Heaven and Earth! The poor common people of Israel scurried from their doomed cities and hid in the caves and the woods.

Only one small band of men, far north in Galilee, gathered their courage to withstand the Philistines. One night they crept to Beth-shan, stole back the bodies of King Saul and his sons and brought them to Jabesh to be buried.

One lone messenger galloped across the southern hills to carry the news down to David at Ziklag. He thought David would be glad for the news. But he was wrong. And his mistake cost him his life.

Chapter 25
The Crown That Would Never Be Lost Again

"He's dead, David. King Saul is dead. Here's his crown."

David fingered the glittering crown and asked in a choked voice, "How do you know he's dead?"

"I killed him myself. I saw he couldn't live. I killed him for you and hurried as fast as I could to tell you. I knew you'd be glad to know your mortal enemy is dead."

The young Amalekite was astonished to see the mighty David bury his head in the crook of his arm and begin to weep. 'Oh, don't tell them in Gath that Saul is dead. Don't publish it in the streets of Askelon. Don't let the Philistines rejoice! And Jonathan! Jonathan is dead. I am distressed for you, my brother Jonathan; very pleasant have you been to me. Your love was wonderful' (II Samuel 1:19–26).

David's men wept with him. Though Saul had been their enemy, they could not rejoice because he was dead. God's anointed king over Israel was dead, dead by the hand of this Amalekite who coolly waited for his reward!

"Weren't you afraid to touch the Lord's anointed?" David raised his head to ask.

The man shrugged. It didn't seem very important.

Everybody knew that God had chosen David to be the new king.

David called sharply to one of his young men. "Kill him. He has killed the king!"

David tried to forget his grief long enough to decide what he ought to do next. Israel was in bondage to the Philistines. They needed a leader desperately. Would they want him to help them? Or had they learned to hate David because Saul hated him? As always, David decided to talk it over with the Lord. "Lord, should I go up to one of the cities of Judah?"

"Yes, David," God answered, "go up."

"Which city, Lord?"

"Hebron."

'Thank You, Lord. You are so good to show me always what I need to do' (Psalm 37:23). With a glad and confident heart, David gave his men moving instructions. They packed their household goods on donkeys and brought their families up from Ziklag to Hebron.

The men of the city heard David was coming. They hurried to meet him. "This is our king!" they shouted. "This is our king!"

But not every town was ready for King David. Across the Jordan River, north at Mahanaim, trouble brewed. For Abner, Saul's general, decided to make Ish-bosheth king. Ish-bosheth was the only son of Saul still alive. All the others had been killed at the battle of Gilboa. He would have been king under ordinary circumstances, for the crown is passed from father to son. But God had said, and Abner should have known, that He had rejected Saul's house and given the crown to David. Nevertheless,

Abner tried to get the men of Israel to follow Ish-bosheth.

David had never lifted his hand against King Saul. He had made a covenant with Jonathan that he would protect the whole family of Saul. So David certainly did not intend to try to kill Ish-bosheth. If God did not unite the hearts of the men of Israel and Judah to make David king, then he wasn't going to try to make himself king!

People couldn't make up their minds. Loyalties seesawed back and forth. Then Abner got mad at Ish-bosheth and went over to David's side. That didn't end the turmoil because Joab, David's nephew and his trusted general, had hated Abner for many years since he'd killed Joab's brother Asahel in a fight. Joab plotted against Abner and secretly murdered him (II Samuel 3:30). David was horrified. Joab had broken David's solemn promise of protection to Abner. Now there was no one to fight for Ish-bosheth, and two men broke into his house and killed him while he slept. Angrily, David commanded their execution (II Samuel 4:12).

Finally the men of Israel realized God had indeed already made David king. From all over the country they gathered to Hebron. "David, we are your bone and flesh. When Saul was king over us, you were the one who led us. God has chosen you for our king. We swear our allegiance to you."

In that holy, solemn moment, every man bowed himself to the ground.

As the priest poured the anointing oil on David's head and it dripped down, David thought of that day so long ago when the prophet Samuel had first anointed him king of Israel. Now, fifteen years later, when David was thirty-three years old, he really was king of all Israel.

The crown sparkled in the sunlight as they placed it on his head. David, the shepherd boy, was the mighty king of Israel. No more would Philistines stalk through the land, stealing and looting and killing. No more would the Amalekites and Moabites rob and burn. Israel had a king, a real king. Under God's leadership, David would lead the armies of Israel to sure victory over every enemy.

But David was not satisfied. There was still one more thing he wanted from God.

"Dear Lord, I love You so much. I want to build a beautiful house for You."

'No, David,' God answered, 'I've chosen something better for you. When you were just a shepherd boy, I chose you to rule My people. I went with you every place you went. I've made your name great. Now, David, I want to promise you one thing more. I promise you an eternal throne—one that will last forever. I won't take the throne away from you, ever, as I did Saul. I promise you that your descendant will sit on this throne forever!' (II Samuel 7:16).

A thousand years later in a small village of Galilee, a young virgin girl listened in awe to the angel who stood before her (Luke 1:26–33).

'Fear not, Mary,' the angel said, 'for you have found favor with God. You will conceive and bring forth a son and shall call his name JESUS. He shall be great and shall be called the Son of the Highest, and the Lord God shall give unto him the throne of his father David, and he shall reign over the house of Jacob forever, and of his kingdom there shall be no end.'

King David, sitting on his throne and peering down through the mists of all the years, understood that one day Jesus would come. By faith he realized that his son Jesus would die for the sins of the world. Then he knew that

Jesus would be crowned King over the whole earth and rule in righteousness and justice. His name would be called Jesus, the Son of David!

Years before, God looked down and saw the child David, a simple shepherd boy. But he was an earnest child, a brave and noble lad. When temptation pressed him from every side, he did what he knew to do. God saw his faith, his holy love, his trustworthiness. God reached down and chose him to be the great king of Israel and forerunner of the Lord Jesus. Through all the wonders and marvels David would see as king through many, many years, the greatest of all marvels was this: God would let Jesus sit on the throne of David—forever!

Publishing the World's Finest Christian Literature

swordofthelord.com